Prai

KNIVES ON THE CUTTING EDGE

"Holding this book you may be asking why Bob Macdonald? I've never heard of this guy? Well, let me tell you that very few people on earth have the comparative experience that Bob has. Putting serious food into perspective necessitates a complete and total comprehensive understanding of the way the world of fine dining works; it requires a serious palate, an educated approach, a personal connection to food and a globalist sensibility. Bob has all that and more. He has dined everywhere, supported real dining and the chefs who make it possible for decades, and is so well-versed that when I needed someone to support me and my efforts to better understand that world Bob was the first one I turned to. Why Bob? Because in a world of poseurs he is the real deal."

Andrew Zimmern, the host and creator of the Travel Channel's *Bizarre Foods America*, *Bizarre World* and *Bizarre Foods with Andrew Zimmern*

"This lover of our art presents what we, actors of the gastronomy, will never be able to see: An in-depth experience of the upscale world of international cooking around the world, and way above that, a vision for tomorrow."

Michel Bras and family, Michelin three-star chef, Bras (Laguiole, France)

"An extraordinary journey through time and gourmandise narrated by a gourmet and gourmand ... This book recounts with passion ... the last two decades, which makes me want to rush into these restaurants."

Pascal Barbot, Michelin three-star chef, L'Astrance (Paris)

"Mr. Macdonald invites us on a wonderful journey from table to table. He sends us his passion for creation and tradition. There is love in what he does."

Michel Troisgros, Michelin three-star chef, La Maison Troisgros (Roanne, France)

"Bob and Sue have reflected in this substantial work two decades of shared passion throughout the most sought after and diverse dining locales in Europe."

Juan Mari & Elena Arzak, Michelin three-star chefs, Arzak (San Sebastian, Spain)

"Through extensive firsthand experience over the course of so many years, Bob and Sue have gathered invaluable reflections on the evolution of fine dining. In *Knives on the Cutting Edge*, they explore the most spectacular restaurants around the world, giving us a thoughtful look into the way we eat today."

Daniel Humm, Michelin three-star chef, Eleven Madison Park (New York City)

Knives on the Cutting Edge

BOB MACDONALD

red portal press

An imprint of SCARLETTA PRESS

SCARLETTA PRESS · MINNEAPOLIS

Copyright © January 2012 Bob Macdonald

Published by Scarletta Press

All rights reserved. No part of this book may be used or reproduced in any manner whatsoever without written permission except in the case of brief quotations embodied in critical articles and reviews. For information, write to Scarletta Press, 10 South Fifth Street #1105, Minneapolis, MN 55402, U.S.A., www.scarlettapress.com.

This book is a work of personal insights. Any opinions stated within are purely those of the author, and not necessarily shared by Scarletta Press. To the best of our knowledge, all names, places, restaurants, and ingredients have been spelled correctly. Any inaccuracies should be reported to Scarletta Press.

Library of Congress Cataloging-in-Publication Data

Macdonald, Bob

Knives on the cutting edge : the great chefs' dining revolution / by Bob Macdonald, Jr.

   p.   cm.

ISBN-13: 978-0-9830219-8-8 (pbk. : alk. paper)
ISBN-10: 0-9830219-8-8 (pbk. : alk. paper)
ISBN-13: 978-0-9830219-9-5 (electronic)
ISBN-10: 0-9830219-9-6 (electronic)

1. Cooking. 2. Cooks—Europe. 3. Cooks—United States. 4. Restaurants. 5. Wine and wine making. 6. Natural foods. I. Title.

TX651.M324 2012
641.5—DC23

                                                    2011053388

Editor: Lisa Wagner
Production Management: Mighty Media
Cover Design: Anders Hanson
Interior Design: Chris Long
Publicity: Desiree Bussiere, desiree@scarlettapress.com

Distributed by Publishers Group West
Printed in Canada

Dedication

*To my wife Sue who shared these wonderful experiences with me,
and to my two sons Scott and Todd who keep me grounded.*

Table of Contents

！◎！

PROLOGUE

Learning to Love Chefs

WE LOVE CHEFS. NOT ONLY ARE THEY THE TRUE ARTISTS OF the current generation, but their creativity and intelligence can provide a dining experience that is, for many of us, the best kind of entertainment. Chefs do not choose an easy lifestyle. Acquiring the proper cooking techniques to become great chefs takes years of working for more experienced chefs who are talented and willing enough to teach them. The newfound and growing respect for chefs in the United States is resulting from the more interesting menus they are developing, as well as their abilities to successfully promote their profession and their own reputations.

Dining is such a personal experience that critics and chefs can vary widely about what they believe is great. Chefs today cannot rest on their laurels but must continue to meet increasingly high standards of excellence; in more difficult times, tremendous pressures exist on chefs at the high-end to remain economically viable—which can mean doing more with less.

Food has become truly international. Asian flavors and cooking techniques are being adopted worldwide, and sophisticated American chefs are taking their place alongside even the greatest European chefs as masters of their trade. The Michelin Red Guides, which have been the standard for recognizing the greatest restaurants, has expanded the countries for which it provides annual ratings to include America and Asia. At the same time, diners are becoming much more interested in selecting their restaurants by the creativity and personality of the chef, and the concept of a celebrity chef is being reinforced through highly visible television shows and best-selling cookbooks.

Never have we had so many interesting dining choices. Comfort food at reasonable prices is now being cooked and offered by many classically trained chefs. Great gourmet cooking has become readily accessible to many more people in the United States—without having to travel to Europe. More chefs are deconstructing food with experimental offerings and cooking techniques that test our knowledge and senses about how food should taste and in what forms food should be served. It is enormously satisfying to participate in a dining revolution that is redefining the entire paradigm of how and what we eat.

This ongoing evolution of hearty comfort food, thoughtful gourmet cooking with finesse, and deconstructed food presented through new textures and unusual flavor combinations (powders, gelatins, foams, frozen foams [air], purees, and ice creams), reflects the desire of chefs to offer uniquely satisfying food experiences in ways that leave their individual signatures. Street food with its spicy flavors has now moved from fast-food menus into mainstream gourmet cooking as diners increasingly crave hotter flavors. It seems that all aspects of the dining spectrum are in continuous evolution and flux, which dedicated eaters find quite exciting.

The sous vide utilize a slow-cooked vacuum concept to provide amazingly tender textures and more concentrated flavors. Liquid nitrogen is being used to reconstruct food ingredients and products into new forms that stimulate our thinking and test the boundaries of creative food preparation. Grilling and cooking in wood-burning and tandoori ovens, smokers, and a la plancha offer other creative and satisfying ways of preparing meat, fish, and vegetables.

Most serious food people grow up in households that put a strong emphasis on tasteful, well-prepared meals and, most importantly, expose them as children to a wide variety of food experiences so they learn to eat everything. My wife Sue and I both had mothers who were excellent cooks so we regularly had delicious comfort food for our meals at home. We started our married life in the late 1960s in New York City where we both developed a love for great food. We would save our money to splurge on memorable lunches at Lutece, and sample a wide range of ethnic restaurants such as Casa Brasil, which introduced us to exotic dishes like Brazilian feijoada (pig's ear stew).

Our first visit to France together in 1970 transformed our interest in food forever after experiencing the three-star restaurants La Tour d'Argent and Paul Bocuse in their primes. We recognized how much more advanced France seemed at the time than the United States, both in appreciating its chef community and in supporting the notion of dining as an evening's pleasure. Yet, in retrospect, these restaurants still represented the old style of French cooking with heavy sauces and less emphasis on fresh ingredients.

Living in Singapore for two and a half years in the early 1970s provided a unique opportunity to sample food from over 200 different restaurants and stalls offering Chinese, Malaysian, Indonesian, Indian, and Korean cuisines, often cooked by expatriate natives from those Asian countries. At the end of our stay, Singapore Airlines published and distributed my restaurant guide to the 100 best eating places, which I titled *Singapore, The Food Capital of Asia*.

Subsequently, while we were raising our family in Seattle and then Minneapolis, our fine dining focused more on Sue's outstanding gourmet meals, accompanied by wines from my growing cellar. When our two sons moved away from home in the early 1990s, family vacations became just the two of us again and we focused more on European travel. After a few years, the idea of visiting all the current three-star restaurants in France (and to a large extent Spain, Italy, the United Kingdom, and the United States) became of interest. We wanted to have benchmarks that would help us understand just how great food could be. This also allowed us to better appreciate our other ongoing dining experiences in the United States.

Our passion for great food and wine now focuses on seeking out those special experiences with old favorites as well as venturing into the unknown at new restaurants we believe will be exciting. Every meal becomes a potential adventure to see what level of creative expression a chef can produce. Experiencing enough of those great meals a year is important, while in between we can focus more on eating healthy low-fat, low-carbohydrate foods and supporting independent local chefs in our Twin Cities community.

With fifty European trips now since 1992, we have managed to eat at least one meal at all twenty-five of the current three-star restaurants in France, including 125 meals at French restaurants that had three stars at the time, and another thirty at restaurants in France that later earned three stars with the same chef. We have had an additional fourteen meals at French restaurants that no longer had three stars (including those with different chefs), and have now eaten at forty-one different restaurants in France that had three stars at some point in time. This has provided us with an invaluable perspective on what should be expected in a three-star experience, and offered insights on some of the recent dramatic changes in the Michelin ratings.

Multiple meals at our French favorites have included Pierre Gagnaire (thirteen) and L'Astrance (nine) in Paris, Michel Bras (eleven) in Laguiole, and Le Bricourt/Le Coquillage (nine) in Cancale. In addition, we have enjoyed twenty meals at three-star restaurants in Spain; fifteen in Italy, Switzerland, and the United Kingdom; and over forty in what are now currently recognized as Michelin three-star restaurants in the United States. Our first-hand experiences with many of these chefs are included in Part One, "Chasing the Michelin Stars." It has been a great ride so far and a hobby we hope to be able to continue to actively enjoy.

To seek out all the three-star restaurants in France really took quite a commitment. It started with our attitude never to "waste a meal" when traveling in France, Spain, or the great food cities of the United States. Our meals in local bistros and even picnics with fresh French bread and favorites such as pork rillettes, sliced sausages and hams, celery remoulade, and Comte cheese could sometimes be just as memorable. Besides, these are really a necessary break from just eating at the "food temples."

A great deal of forethought and planning are required on the front end, to ensure that every reservation we are seeking can be secured, and to be certain that each is properly reconfirmed. So we have used most of my twenty vacation days a year to travel and seek out great eating experiences that I record with meticulous notes and pass along with the menus to more than forty chefs and friends around the United States. Since November 2007, we have also been posting highlights of our trips on our "Bob and Sue's Culinary Adventures" blog at Andrew-Zimmern.com. Hopefully, these summaries of our favorite meals are useful to people planning visits to those cities.

Restaurant Reservations

While reservations at some of the greatest restaurants in the world (elBulli, Noma, Fat Duck, etc.) can be almost impossible to obtain, it is still worth trying. In Paris and other major cities, a topflight hotel often has the clout to get its guests into those food shrines. To minimize chances for disappointment, reservations should be attempted three to nine months ahead of the anticipated visit, although many restaurants have strict rules about not taking reservations until one or two months before the date requested. Sending a fax or an e-mail with a personal note is another approach some restaurants will honor.

Once you have visited a restaurant it is sometimes easier to get in a second time, especially if you have followed up with a thoughtful thank you note or made a connection with the front of the house. When visiting a great chef, we often bring a gift of a domestic wine to show our appreciation for his or her talents. This sometimes invites a brief interaction with the chef, which enriches the dining experience. (The wines must be packed in bubble wrap and checked as luggage to comply with today's travel restrictions on liquids.)

While we always try to have at least one "great" eating experience a day (and therefore have not been fans of joining bicycle or barge excursions in France), we also get great satisfaction out of visiting art museums and cathedrals, and driving through scenic countryside during the day. With the large amount of food we tend to consume, it is important to find time for regular exercise, which is primarily a lot of walking whenever possible.

Our kids think we are more than a little obsessive, but they have been increasingly enjoying these trips when they are invited to join us. The special food and wines, as well as the great sites they have experienced, are all part of our family legacy now. It would not be surprising to see them carry on many of these types of experiences with their own children some day, as their appreciation for great dining experiences grows every year.

Although we speak and understand only a limited amount of French, this has not seemed to slow us down too much. Often the language differences have been a part of the fun. A brochure we found at an Alain Ducasse-owned hotel in the French Pyrenees town of Biddaray in the heart of the Basque country is a great example. While enjoying breathtaking views of sheep filled hillsides and dining on local gastronomic specialties such as wild river salmon and a unique dark brown potato, we had a chuckle when the promotional brochure describing this magical place as *"egalement une halte gourmande per ses hotes"* was translated into English as "a greedy halt for its hosts."

In addition to these unbelievable European trips, we were continuing to do long weekends in our favorite US food capitals such as New York, San Francisco, Chicago, and New Orleans. We appreciated how dramatically the latest generation of chefs had raised the bar since 1990 and the many incredible dining adventures that resulted from their creativity and constantly evolving techniques. In the early 1990s, such chefs as Charlie Trotter in Chicago and Wolfgang Puck in Los Angeles and San Francisco were causing quite a stir with their innovative menus and food presentations that made dining so much more exciting. The gap was narrowing between the US chefs and the greatest chefs of Europe as they began influencing each other's cooking techniques and choice of ingredients across country boundaries.

Recently, a clear trend has emerged toward more informal dining, and tablecloths are disappearing along with strict dress codes. People are increasingly seeking out seats at counters overlooking an open kitchen. Lower price points reflect menus with simpler, comfort food choices that are attracting new diners who want more than fast food from chains. Food trucks are becoming an alternative to fast-food restaurants for lunch.

Ambiance in many restaurants has increasingly come to mean having a properly trained and highly attentive wait staff. As our son Todd, who is a classically trained chef and has cooked in San Francisco, Boston, and most recently New York City points out, "A restaurant is only as good as the front of the house. If the waiters and sommeliers let you down, it does not matter how good the food is, because the dining experience will not be special."

While not everyone dining in a restaurant is there to appreciate the wine, we view wine as an integral part of the overall dining experience. Over forty years of serious collecting and drinking many of the greatest wines made in the twentieth century have reinforced our appreciation for its importance to the pleasure of a great meal. An attentive sommelier can add much to a meal by sharing his or her insights into a well-chosen list. On the other hand, a sommelier can also seriously spoil the enjoyment of a meal by the way he or she attempts to "protect" the wine list or by failing to build a representative, fairly priced collection to support the level of the food. Part Two, "Meeting Grape Expectations," offers a brief journey through some of the great wines we have shared with others and by which we educated ourselves, and includes many of our best and worst restaurant wine experiences.

Part Three, "Megatrends," explores some interesting developments involving the current production and consumption of food that merit our attention. The healthfulness of the food we eat quite properly is an area of increasing concern as we become more aware of the importance of fat and carbohydrate contents, the linking of foods to specific diseases, the necessity to consume at least minimum amounts of proteins and vitamins, and the many benefits of eating the more natural, organic foods that are often sustainable and locally grown. I need to heed some of this advice myself with my attachment to such unhealthy foods as White Castle hamburgers and snacks like Nacho Cheese Bugles and wasabi-covered peas.

This recent emphasis on seeking out sustainable locally grown food does not appear to be a passing fad. With the greater time being spent in fast food and other low-cost chain restaurants (because people have less time to cook meals at home), an awareness of the current and long-term consequences many of these menu choices may have on our health becomes increasingly important.

The outlook for independent, chef-driven restaurants in the United States is another area of increasing concern. As celebrity chefs establish their multiple-restaurant corporate empires of higher-end cooking in parallel to the growth of fast-food chains, independent, chef-driven neighborhood restaurants may have increasing difficulty competing at equivalent price points and achieving the same level of visibility and success in the battle for consumers' limited dollars. The ratio of our most capable young chefs working for these growing corporate entities is likely to increase, leaving fewer chefs willing to take on the higher risks associated with staying independent to go it alone. Independent neighborhood chefs have often been the primary sources of new ideas that are vital to ensuring creative menus will be developed in the future.

The role of peppers and many other spices and hot sauces in achieving bolder flavors is another important megatrend worth noting. Spices are increasingly having an influence on gourmet cooking, which traditionally has emphasized more subtle flavors in its classic dishes.

Highlighting the contributions of those chefs who have had the greatest impact in elevating great cooking over the last two decades is particularly relevant during this time of evolving ideas about food. While people will have differing opinions based on their own dining preferences, I like to break down today's chefs into three primary categories: 1) the deconstructionists; 2) the classic gourmet chefs; and 3) the great comfort food chefs often found in French bistros, Italian trattorias, and other leading ethnic restaurants.

Among the notable deconstructionists, Ferran Adria in Spain, Heston Blumenthal in England, and Grant Achatz in Chicago will be discussed in Part One. Any current list of the classically trained gourmet chefs who push the envelope and deserve their current reputations for greatness should include Pierre Gagnaire and Pascal Barbot in Paris, Michel Bras in Laguiole, Alain Ducasse in Monte Carlo, Marc Veyrat in Annecy, Thomas Keller in the United States, and Tetsuya Wakuda in Sydney, Australia. Masa Takayama in New York has been redefining sushi dining in the United States, while Rick Bayless in Chicago has introduced US diners to great traditional Mexican comfort food. As many of these great chefs now approach retirement with less involvement in their kitchens, a new generation of chefs is emerging to make their own marks as the future leaders of their profession. Many seem to be embracing the art of cooking comfort food well, which means less emphasis on great gourmet cooking.

There are those who think we are coming to the end of the era in which Michelin stars are the primary way of evaluating greatness. As the Michelin Red Guides struggle to maintain financial viability, a new Nordic cooking movement is capturing the imagination of chefs around the world. Originating with the Copenhagen restaurant Noma, which has headed the S.Pelligrino World's Best 50 Restaurants list since 2010, its "return to the basic ingredients" approach is already achieving serious credibility as a real force in creative cuisine.

We did not begin these culinary pilgrimages with the objective of some day putting our experiences into a book, but over the past two decades, planning trips to ensure meaningful food and wine adventures every day just became something we loved doing. It was the recent realization that very few people may have ever visited so many of the greatest restaurants in the world that made me decide it might be interesting to share these stories with other foodies and wine lovers with similar passions. It has been particularly exciting to see how more diners have become avid supporters of innovative chefs in every country that is serious about its food.

On our food adventures, we usually show up at these legendary culinary temples without any special introduction. We try to observe why they are considered unique—either through their cooking styles or those signature dishes that make them so special. We have now become friends with a number of chefs and maître d's in France, Spain, and the United States, and enjoy exchanging Christmas and New Year's cards between our visits.

We feel very fortunate to have had the time and means to make these trips, and to be able to acquire so many really special food and wine memories. We have room to highlight only a small number of the many wonderful restaurants we have visited in Europe and the US. This book is a tribute to the great chefs of the last two decades in Europe and the United States, so their contributions might be remembered and more fully appreciated. We may look back at the period from 1990 to the present as a unique time of unprecedented advances in cooking techniques. We are pleased to share many of the anecdotes and fun stories about the innovative and dedicated restaurant people who have been living on the cutting-edge of this amazing dining revolution.

PART I

Chasing the Michelin Stars

ᵰ◎ᵰ

CHAPTER 1

The Importance of the Third Star

EARNING THREE MICHELIN STARS IS THE AMBITION OF MOST great French chefs throughout their careers, because three stars is a recognition that very few ever achieve. It does mean instant respect from fellow chefs, especially in France, which has a long history of being a country with passionate and committed diners. And this is also true to some extent in Switzerland, Spain, Italy, England, Germany, Belgium, and the Netherlands where the Michelin Guides have long recognized the greatest restaurants.

The Michelin Red Guides have not been without controversy in recent years, however, as some chefs now voluntarily give back their stars and a chef committed suicide in 2003 when he believed he might lose his third star. Yet despite its recent financial problems, the guide has remained the standard for measuring greatness over the last 100 years in France. Other sources such as the Gault Millau guide and annual Top 50 lists (such as that offered by S. Pellegrino) add to our knowledge and provide other perspectives that are gaining increasing credibility.

The sadness that occurs when a third Michelin star is taken away is hard for most Americans to fathom. A few very deserving French chefs get their third star back, like Jacques Lameloise in Chagny or Jean Michel Lorain at Côte Saint Jacques in Joigny. But for some, including Roger Verget of Moulin de Mougins outside Cannes, it is never regained before the chef retires and sells his restaurant to the next generation.

On our only visit to Moulin de Mougins in September 1993

(shortly after Verget had been downgraded from three stars to two), he approached our table after a particularly enjoyable classical lobster presentation. When I complimented him for serving a perfect course, there seemed to be melancholy and sadness in his voice as he replied, "It has to be."

MICHELIN STARS

Michelin awards its stars annually in each country (or city, in the United States) for which it publishes a Red Guide after analyzing the dining comments of anonymous, professional reviewers; every restaurant has been visited one or more times by a Michelin reviewer. This is not a popularity contest by the general public. Every year new restaurants achieve the highest three-star rating or become one- or two-star restaurants for the first time. These announcements are much anticipated by gourmet diners who eagerly follow changes in these ratings. Other restaurants are demoted by having stars taken away when food quality declines.

While three stars are awarded for achieving the highest quality food of its type, other factors such as atmosphere, level of service, and even quality of the plates, glassware, and cutlery, can also have an influence. For more than 100 years, the Michelin Red Guides have been the standard for recognizing where to have the most memorable dining experiences.

Olivier Roellinger's Third Star

Each year in the late fall, after our two or three trips to Europe are completed, it has become my routine to write a letter to Michelin summarizing our various experiences, with a special emphasis on France. In 2005, we had enjoyed another outstanding meal at Olivier Roellinger's restaurant in Cancale, "the oyster capital of the world," on the Breton coast. Roellinger had been a highly respected two star-chef for eighteen years, and we felt he deserved some special attention in the letter. His definitive book on the history of spices features extraordinary color photographs and insights into how each spice can best be used. His thoughtful seafood appetizers are likely to include not only the freshest local Breton oysters but creative preparations of raw scallops, John Dory sashimi, or a memorable spider crab served in an avocado cream with ginger and crab mustard sauce. Roellinger was one of the first French chefs to incorporate Asian spices into many of his appetizers and main courses, including his legendary signature lobster preparations.

With no three-star chefs in Brittany and the acknowledged reverence with which he was regarded by his fellow chefs throughout France, it seemed to be long overdue for Roellinger to finally receive his third star. Our six visits beginning in 1992 had only reinforced this idea for us. I spent extra time crafting the Michelin letter that fall and sent Roellinger a copy. When the Michelin awards were announced in early 2006, Roellinger was the only new three-star chef selected in all of France. We sent a congratulatory fax expressing how excited we were for him and his dedicated wife Jane. In the press, Roellinger was quoted as saying his new star provided "a very, very intense joy and a victory for seafood." He had the impression that the Michelin Guides were more for "the cuisine of meat lovers." This is an interesting comment, since he served a wonderful saddle of the pré salé lamb (lamb that grazes on the nearby salt marshes). It is one of the most memorable tableside carved meat courses we have ever enjoyed, featuring a unique and subtle salty aftertaste in the lamb.

Roellinger's restaurant is truly elegant in an understated way. The service is flawless and hardly noticeable—the sign of proper coordination between the kitchen and front of the house. The center dining room looks out on a pond where ducks are swimming and napping.

We had planned a trip to Paris in mid-March 2006 as part of Sue's birthday celebration with Nancy and Bruce Thomson, her sister and brother-in-law, and were fortunate that Roellinger had decided to reopen that week from his winter closing. We did not know what to expect from our visit on only his fourth day of operation after receiving the coveted third star. Roellinger is a modest chef who seldom leaves his kitchen to interact with his diners, and we had never met him in person on any of our previous visits.

As we entered the alcove of the restaurant, we were surprised to see Roellinger waiting for us. His words in broken English were, "Bob, you were there when we needed you. Part of this third star is yours." We know my letter was not the primary reason for his elevation since he expressed similar gratitude to his other supporters, but this still was a special moment for all of us to share. Michelin later sent me a personal letter specifically acknowledging my letter supporting Roellinger for his third star.

That evening, Sue brought along a four-inch Baccarat crystal star in a shiny red Baccarat bag and handed it to Roellinger. The enclosed card read, "*La troisième étoile est le meilleur*" (The third star is the best). This was a big hit in the kitchen several minutes later when he opened it in front of his staff. In 2008, Roellinger voluntarily gave up his three stars because he did not want to have to live with the ongoing pressure to maintain this high level of perfection and, most importantly, he had already achieved what meant so much to him. He still maintains an excellent seafood restaurant Coquillage at the site of his attractive, small luxury hotel, Le Richelieu, just outside Cancale.

Roellinger, while a university student, was badly beaten by a gang of thugs. He was twenty years old at the time. During his two-year convalescence, he began cooking and decided to dedicate his life to becoming a chef. Since closing down his gourmet restaurant, Roellinger has focused on his small bistro seafood restaurant, a bakery, an interesting spice-oriented grocery, and a cooking school.

We have continued to enjoy the dramatic ocean views around Cancale, which are accented by the strongest tides in the world, on our regular trips to this beautiful area of Northern Brittany (with Mont Saint-Michel occasionally visible across the water on the horizon). We especially look forward to buying the Breton plate and cruise oysters from the female vendors located along the seawall on the edge of downtown Cancale near the oyster beds. The sweetness of these freshly caught oysters is always special, and many people, including ourselves, consider Breton oysters to be the greatest in the world. Plus, it is always fun to toss the shells back into the ocean from the edge of the seawall when we are finished eating.

CHAPTER 2

The Legends of Modern Cooking

Jöel Robuchon

Perhaps, the greatest three-star meal I have ever eaten in my life was in Paris at Jöel Robuchon's namesake restaurant in March 1996, about six months before he retired from a full-time role in the kitchen to do consulting. Even the fact that I had the worst seat in the restaurant that day, facing nothing but a wall, could not spoil the enjoyment of this unforgettable meal. Each of the beautifully presented and perfectly cooked courses is still a vivid memory. My favorite course was the lobster served under vermicelli noodles perfectly wrapped in a spiral, accompanied by a delicious lobster sauce and sliced black truffles. Every bite was magical.

Even a simple sliced green apple with Iranian caviar was stunning in the hands of this master. Robuchon's legendary mashed potatoes made with more than abundant amounts of butter and cream were the perfect accompaniment to the rare pigeon wrapped in savoy cabbage. Robuchon seldom left his kitchen, and the continuing pressure of his obsessive dedication to perfection may have been the reason he finally decided to retire as a full-time chef while still very much in his prime.

Before retiring in 1996 at age fifty-one, Robuchon had been named "Chef of the Century" by Gault Millau. Even though Robuchon has now returned to the restaurant world and put his name on several fine dining endeavors, as well as his counter-oriented L'Atelier de Joël Robuchon in Paris, London, New York, Las Vegas, and Hong Kong, it is the Robuchon of the 1990s who gets my vote as perhaps the greatest chef who ever lived!

His twelve restaurants opened over the past decade have accumulated twenty-seven total Michelin stars (including three stars in Las Vegas, Tokyo, and Hong Kong)—more than any other chef in the world. His attitude has always been there is no such thing as a perfect meal—a chef should always strive to do better in making each ingredient taste the way it was meant to taste. Robuchon tries to accentuate two or three flavors in each dish rather than to create unusual combinations of ingredients.

Born in Poitiers, France, Robuchon began cooking at age fifteen in a hotel kitchen as a pastry chef. He served as a chef for the Tour de France, which exposed him to many regional foods before he put Jamin restaurant on the map in Paris.

Ferran Adrià

The chef who is acknowledged as having the greatest influence on cooking in the world over the past decade has been Ferran Adrià of the remotely located elBulli on the Costa Brava coast of Spain. He ended his spectacular run by closing mid-2011. The much-acclaimed father of deconstructionism and molecular gastronomy, Adrià came up with ideas that were so over the top that he changed how we think about food. One did not go to elBulli just to have a normal meal. Rather it was to have a dining experience unlike anything else in the world.

Adrià closed for six months every year from October first to April first to work on innovations for the following year. His recipes often deconstructed classic Spanish and other traditional cuisines, and he is credited with inventing creative ways to present flavors and textures through the use of foams, gelatins, powders, and air (frozen foam). Adrià experimented with food textures, temperatures, and flavor combinations, and also stimulated our senses with new ways in which food could be visualized.

With Adrià, things are not always as they seem. This worked especially well for people who love food and went to his restaurant ready to have fun. His sense of humor was often expressed in many whimsical ways. A reservation at elBulli became almost impossible to obtain, with more than two million annual requests for about 8,000 total seats made available for dinner in the six-month season. So when Adrià announced his intention to close down to pursue other food-related research, it was as if he wanted to preserve a time in culinary history where his creativity never waned.

On our first visit in 2000, when elBulli was still serving lunch as well, we enjoyed twenty-one courses over four hours. It was immediately obvious how much thought had gone into every course in order to make a statement. A traditional Spanish black rice dish was in fact made of chopped bean sprouts colored with squid ink. Although I am definitely not a vegetarian, I found a course of powdered yogurt, olive ice, and balsamic vinegar gelatin cubes in a beet soup to be a particularly satisfying and a memorable combination of flavors and textures. A rarely experienced blowfish offering was served with Swedish calyx caviar. The rack of rabbit in a foie gras sauce came with warm apple gelatin, and a yeast soup was paired with quail eggs and lemon crisps.

The most memorable course (which has now been duplicated by a number of chefs) was the simple hot and cold pea soup with mint. Served in a shot glass, the soup was hot on top and cold on the bottom. We commented about how much the pea flavor changed as we drank it down in several continuous swallows. The entire dining experience was made particularly special by a phone call to Sue halfway through the meal from Elena Arzak of the Arzak restaurant in San Sebastian whose father Juan Mari is a close friend of Adrià.

We had a completely different experience on our second visit to elBulli in 2004, accompanied by our two sons. The entertaining nature of the twenty-six courses had been expanded to include some special packaging of the food for several of the courses. "Air Bulli" arrived in a plain white cardboard box the size of a boxed airline meal. It contained a delicious frozen cheese foam to be eaten with a plastic spoon and was topped with apple and strawberry chips and nuts. For another course, a round metal caviar tin was filled with tiny melon balls to resemble red caviar. The razor clams in ponzu foam were served on top of finely chopped clams that resembled sushi rice, and a deconstructed raw pumpkin gnocchi was served with pumpkin seed oil. A translucent macaroni was accompanied by morels and fresh lychees in a morel sauce, followed by sea cucumber with ham, yogurt jelly, and citrus cubes.

The seven desserts included chocolate ravioli with eucalyptus ice cream, and a macaroon foam sandwich with lime and rose sugars designed to spill all over the table. The final dessert course was an inflated white plastic surgical glove on a round-bottomed metal bowl. The bowl was filled with chocolate-covered corn nuts and could be tipped to rock back and forth, allowing the glove to wave goodbye at the end of the meal. On both visits, we were treated to kitchen tours to greet Adrià, who was a very gracious host.

Adrià's retirement came before he turned fifty, but he had been at elBulli since 1984 and became executive chef there after only eighteen months. To achieve his dramatic contrasts in flavor, temperature, and texture, Adrià freely utilized colorants, gelling agents, emulsifiers, acidifiers, and taste enhancers that were not always the healthiest ingredients. This father of deconstructionist cooking was even asked to teach a culinary physics course at Harvard.

Alain Ducasse

Alain Ducasse has probably done more to promote French cooking around the world than any other living chef. Building on his two initial three-star restaurants in Monte Carlo and Paris, Ducasse has also opened several highly attractive inns in the French countryside in smaller cities such as La Celle, Moustiers-Saint Marie, and Biddaray, as well as bistros in Paris, New York, and Tokyo. In addition, he has developed major restaurants at The Dorchester in London (rated three stars since 2010) and the St. Regis hotels in New York; Washington, DC; and London; as well as recently taking over the Jules Verne restaurant on the second level of the Eiffel Tower. Ducasse is also the author of *Le Grand Livre de Cuisine*, the most definitive French cookbook ever written, which is so large it should be priced by the pound.

Ducasse's original restaurant, Louis XV in Monte Carlo, where he earned his first three stars in 1990, remains our personal favorite by far. With ornate paintings on the gilded walls and ceiling, and overlooking a square with its opulent casino and jet-set cars, this is one of the most beautiful settings for a meal in the entire world. Coupled with impeccable service and many special touches (including upholstered purse holders and separate carts for bread and coffee/tea service), Louis XV delivers a dining experience that always makes one feel special. Ducasse has really been out of his kitchen here since the mid-1990s attending to his growing restaurant empire, so it has been his chef de cuisine, Franck Cerutti, who has been responsible for ensuring that the highest quality ingredients are used and the flavors are memorable.

A wonderful menu selection of seafood, meat, and vegetarian courses makes choosing very difficult. The bold Mediterranean flavors of the shellfish in a seafood broth, morel risotto with baby wild green asparagus, and pigeon in a blood sauce with hot foie gras reflect his cooking roots as well as the touch of a classic master chef. And finishing every meal with a simple frais du bois (wild strawberries) with mascarpone ice cream becomes a perfect accent point for me. Our five visits here have been equally memorable, with no drop-off in the attention to details, which is the hallmark of great service. It was hard to understand at the time why the Michelin Guide twice briefly took away his third star in Monte Carlo, where Ducasse's heart and soul are always so obviously on display. The Guide may have felt he was spreading himself too thin by opening the new restaurants in his name in Paris and then New York City.

We had the opportunity to eat our first al fresco lunch there on a gorgeous, sunny day in September 2010. The view from the patio overlooking the casino and the crowds of tourists—with the occasional Ferrari—has to be one of the most pleasant spots in the world. We were treated to an exceptional meal that included many of our old favorites, plus a delicious green herb-infused pasta with cooked and raw cèpes and sea bass in black olive sauce.

It also provided the chance to drink the incredible 2002 Coche Dury Meursault-Perrières with this perfectly cooked food. The giant wooden bread cart offered many different loaves to be sliced (the sun-dried tomato bread was exceptional), and the tea and coffee cart at the end of the meal was a particularly elegant touch not usually available in even the greatest restaurants in the world. To us, Louis XV defines what a three-star restaurant should offer at its best. Combined with flawless service, Louis XV is simply unforgettable.

We found Ducasse's other restaurants in Paris and New York (the latter is now closed, and he has reopened as Adour in the St. Regis Hotel) to be much more formulaic and less inspirational than Monte Carlo, although both earned three Michelin stars as well. In Paris, the service seems almost condescending to a nonnative. Unfortunately, the wine experiences at both these restaurants put a real damper on our meals (discussed in Part Two). While the food at both locations was still of Ducasse quality, our overall dining experience did not leave us with the same "wow" that Louis XV in Monte Carlo always delivers.

Ducasse began cooking at age sixteen and apprenticed under other three-star chefs at the time, such as Michel Guérard and Roger Verget. After surviving a plane crash in 1984, he came to the Hotel de Paris in 1986, put down roots in Monaco, and became a citizen. With twenty-four restaurants around the world, Ducasse is constantly on the go to stay in touch with his culinary empire and enjoy his passion for great wines.

Pierre Gagnaire

For many years, my favorite chef in the world has been Pierre Gagnaire in Paris. He launched his career in his hometown of Saint-Étienne west of Lyon and earned three stars there. This effort failed (due to the high fixed costs) after moving into an ultramodern building in a city that was too far away from the critical mass of gourmet tourists essential to sustain success. Gagnaire's rebirth several years later in 1996 at the Hotel Balzac as the darling of Paris was welcomed by us all. He has continued to walk a balance between pushing the envelope with new and creative food ideas and paying tribute to classical cooking techniques.

Gagnaire absolutely dazzled us during our first visit to Saint-Étienne in 1993. The pastel-colored walls of the futuristic dining room featured round portholes facing into the kitchen. He began by putting seven plates of delicious amuses in front of us before the regular meal even began. No other chef in the world was doing this at the time, and it really grabbed our attention.

On our second visit in 1994, we saw Gagnaire the perfectionist at work when he swooped in on an adjacent table and removed all the plates before anyone had a chance to take a bite of the course. One of the presentations was apparently not just the way he thought it should be. The diners waited twenty minutes before all the plates reappeared again. Among the many memorable courses in Saint-Étienne were sweetbreads stuffed with calamari, langoustines in a beef bouillon tapioca, and lamb from three different regions prepared in creatively different ways on one plate.

In Paris, we have enjoyed eleven additional meals with Gagnaire including a period in the late 1990s when his focus was on offal (organ meat). We have also experienced a twenty-five-year-old oyster cooked with Spanish ham, and a baby eel in garlic butter course that I found to be sheer perfection at the time. For years, we ordered his tasting menus to try to experience as many of his creative courses as possible. Some of the most memorable individual dishes included rabbit quenelles with kidney and foie gras (1997); rabbit shoulder, leg, kidney, and heart with parsnip puree (1999); sea bass with foie gras and turnip cooked in artichoke juice (2001); asparagus, pork ears, and sliced squid with curried asparagus juice (2002); and cream of duck liver en gelée on green lentils with baby artichokes and fried zucchini strips (2003).

In recent visits, we have tried the à la carte selections (which offer five or six interesting small plate variations presented together) with an order of one of our favorite foods such as langoustines, lamb, or duck. Gagnaire continues to be a trendsetter in featuring certain vegetables, meats, and seafood before other chefs—who then often follow his lead. His has been one of the few great restaurants open on a Sunday night in Paris with the chef in the kitchen—something we really appreciate. We have enjoyed taking several US chefs to Gagnaire as our guests, and this has usually been one of the greatest culinary experiences of their lives. Gagnaire has also successfully opened a London restaurant, Sketch, which we believe rivals anything else in that city for great gourmet food.

Gagnaire puts "emotion on the plate" and is inspired by everything from Hermes perfume to Jackson Pollock paintings. While always quite respectful of culinary traditions, he has never been hesitant to experiment with new approaches to flavors, tastes, textures, and ingredients. His chef de cuisine in Las Vegas described this unique cooking approach, "Like flying in a hot air balloon—Gagnaire is the balloon and we are all in the basket following him."

Michel Bras

A visit to Michel Bras near Laguiole in the Aubrac region of central France is always a special experience. This is Sue's favorite restaurant in the world and the site of my most memorable meal, which was on the night of my sixtieth birthday. The dramatic glass and steel restaurant with attractive guest rooms built on a hilltop offer breathtaking views of the town below and the Pyrenees Mountains in the distance. Room 11 is a particular favorite, offering a 180-degree panoramic view and an inviting patio on which to take in the surrounding scenery with a glass of Champagne. Laguiole is also known for the special knives and corkscrews it manufactures and exports throughout the world. One particular factory on the road from the town of Laguiole to Bras is marked by a horizontal "V" on the roof; it deserves its reputation for being the best quality producer in the region and is open to the public most days for shopping at competitive prices.

The understated elegance of Michel Bras' restaurant only adds to the special quality of this remote country setting. The tasting menu is a must-have and can be complemented by a thoughtfully chosen list of great French wines. Michel Bras is now passing the torch to his son Sebastian without any noticeable change in quality, and both their wives are wonderful front-of-the-house ambassadors. Open only six months a year from April through October, this has become an essential pilgrimage for any serious foodie.

Among the several signature dishes are Bras' famous gargouillou of twenty-five to thirty vegetables and herbs that are stunning in their freshness and subtle flavors. Bras grows over 300 different vegetables in his garden. The meat served for the main course varies by season and might include lamb from the Aubrac region. The "Laguiole Potatoes," which were developed originally by Michel's mother and are still prepared by her occasionally, are half potato, half Laguiole cheese. They are served about five minutes into the main course. The potatoes are so dense, they can be held upside down on the spoon with which they are served. Bras is also believed to have invented the liquid-center chocolate cake.

In our nine visits there, we have experienced perfection and many great memories. When Bras received his third star in March 1999, we were so thrilled that we sent a fax offering our congratulations for this well-deserved recognition. It was special on our next visit in the fall of 1999 when Madame Bras (Ginette) told us that of all the congratulations Michel had received, ours "meant the most to him," because it was so unexpected. His first cookbook, *Le Livre de Michel Bras*, published only in French, is extremely hard to find today and remains one of our most treasured souvenirs.

On our October 2009 visit, we had our most memorable main course: a perfectly cooked, single thick slice of rare wild duck breast with a subtle giblet reduction sauce on pureed white quince and served with a baby turnip and juniper berries. We knew it really was wild when Sue found a small piece of buckshot in her slice of duck.

We stayed two nights for the first time in September 2011. After enjoying the wonderful tasting menu the first night, we ordered à la carte and loved the slow-baked onion with truffled bread crumbs on top, the sautéed calamari with an orange tomato sauce, the grilled lobster with a unique citrus vinaigrette, and an exceptional rare-cooked Aubrac beef with truffle sauce.

Bras learned to cook from his mother and has deep roots in this remote Aubrac region where he has lived his entire life. The rustic beauty and basic tastes enjoyed by the people here have clearly defined the cooking style of this "chef's chef."

Marc Veyrat

Marc Veyrat, who had earned a reputation as the enfant terrible of French chefs, struggled to stay out of bankruptcy despite charging some of the highest prices in France for his food and rooms. In March 2009, at age fifty-eight, he announced he was giving up his three stars for health reasons. He became the first French chef ever to hold multiple three-star ratings at the same time—for his restaurants in Annecy and Megève (now closed). At his original (and sole-remaining) restaurant on Lake Annecy in the French alps, Veyrat enjoyed breaking all the rules of traditional French cooking, sometimes serving food from test tubes and syringes to add to the drama of the presentation. Known for foraging his herbs from the nearby hillsides, Veyrat is a true character who delivers delicious and satisfying food along with his innovative presentations.

Veyrat's pinecone floating in consommé was an early signature dish. It was so good, our son Scott once asked for a second bowl, and they happily obliged. Tableside presentations meant to shock have included pouring a seafood broth through a funnel onto a fish with char-burned scales, and serving a truffled egg dish on a thick bed of moss while injecting a green oxalis herb into the egg with a syringe. His deconstructed ravioli with pureed peas and cheese pasta was delicious, and his tarte de flotte featured ham, cheese, and potato foams served in a milk carton. We have never experienced another chef in France who can match the perfection of his classical, simple presentation of hot and cold foie gras on one plate. His foie gras sorbet was also memorable, and a flowerless cheese pasta dissolved completely in ten seconds when a hot chicken consommé was added, leaving a perfectly clear liquid soup. Guests are often asked to guess the flavors of the crème brûlées and sorbets.

On all three of our visits there when we probably should have ordered the substantial fourteen-course menu, we have opted for his twenty-plus "symphony" of courses. This always includes the local "king of the lake" fish from the adjacent Lake Annecy. Several times I have had to volunteer to eat others' portions of this tribute to his hometown (along with the accompanying mushroom sauce from a tube on the third visit), so as not to disappoint the kitchen about this very average-tasting fish. Our family still jokes about the challenge of finding ways to make the "king of the lake" disappear. I love the expression on Sue's face whenever "king of the lake" is mentioned, since she is not an avid eater of some cooked fish. And hands down, Veyrat offers what may be the greatest breakfast spread in the world, which includes incredible selections of fruits, breads, cheeses, meats, fish, and truffled scrambled eggs.

Veryat seems to invite controversy, starting with the time he was expelled from school for setting fire to a teacher. And he has always done things his way—using roots, plants, mountain herbs, and wild flora to flavor his dishes in place of butter, eggs, oils, and creams. Veryat is proud of his heritage from a long line of Savoie mountain peasants, which is why he chose to wear a black shepherd's hat instead of a chef's toque in his kitchen and around the restaurant.

Pascal Barbot

The future of French food in Paris may be found in the creative menus of Pascal Barbot at L'Astrance on the right bank across the Seine from the Eiffel Tower. This comfortable restaurant with only twenty-five seats was originally opened in 2000 after Barbot (who was sous chef to Alain Passard) and maître d' Christophe Rohat left the three-star L'Arpege to develop their own special place at a more attractive price point. L'Astrance earned its first star after only six months and by 2007 had amazingly reached its third star, in the same year when more formal, established food churches such as Taillevant and George Cinq lost their third stars. Not surprisingly, Barbot was chosen Chef of the Year in France by the Gault Millau guide for 2005. Barbot and Rohat were genuinely touched by each additional star, stating that they were determined not to change their approach, even as their recognition grew.

Barbot's early signature dishes included non-pasta ravioli that featured avocado slices filled with crab or raw mushroom slices layered with foie gras. Diners are sometimes asked to guess the flavor of the ice creams presented (toast ice cream was one of the more unusual ones). The menu, which is never written, changes regularly to reflect the best seasonal offerings. All meat and fish are cooked on the bone. Other memorable dishes during our visits have included hot lobster with brioche crumbs, and leg of veal with Spanish ham prosciutto, Parmesan puree, eggplant, and miso glaze. Sue's sixtieth-birthday lunch included raw scallops in a shrimp consommé, celery soup with pureed black truffles and hazelnut oil, and pigeon and abalone slices in the same bowl with a special herbed broth.

While we have been dedicated fans of L'Astrance from our first meal, we were not expecting the special menu Pascal prepared for us on our October 2010 visit. He had spent some time in the Far East during his summer vacation that year and surprised us with a dazzling poached lobster served with delicious satay sauce and a crunchy chile pepper roll. In fact, the five courses served in the middle of the meal were so creative and delicious, that by the end I proclaimed it one of the two best meals of my life.

Pascal paired a perfectly cooked turbot with a tamarind and dry raisin sauce, topped with squid and a red pepper powder and accompanied by razor clams with garlic butter and thyme. Next came a Bresse chicken breast with a sauce of creamy Parmesan and sliced white truffles, and raw and cooked cèpes. A wild Marais duck was paired with red and green cabbage, a sour cherry Brazilian sweet chili, and duck liver on toast. A wild hare followed in red wine sauce with chocolate, yuzu, rosemary, and thyme. And dessert included a pear velouté and chile pepper ice cream with lemongrass. One of these courses alone would have been a great memory.

Rohat and sommelier Alexandre Jean (Gault Millau's 2009

Best Sommelier in France) oversee a reasonably priced, thoughtful wine list that they will supplement occasionally with some special gems tucked away in the cellar. The service is understated but highly efficient, and the seamless coordination between the kitchen and front of the house is one of the reasons L'Astrance always feels like such a special experience. L'Astrance is named after a hearty, non-edible wild flower native to Europe that is often dried and used for decoration.

Growing up in Vichy in the Auvergne region of Central France where he helped his father harvest vegetables, Barbot had decided by age seven that he wanted to become a chef. His mentor, Alain Passard at L'Arpege, taught him to respect the natural flavors of products and has been a great influence on his cooking. Barbot is known for the thoughtful combinations he brings together in dishes which are complementary in ways that might not occur to most chefs. In the highly competitive Paris restaurant scene, Barbot has carved out a unique niche for himself by not being bound in his thinking by traditional conventions.

ᵼ🍽ᵼ

CHAPTER 3
Other Paris Three-Star Chefs

Bernard Pacaud

L'Ambroisie on the Place des Vosges offers a memorable—even romantic—experience that we often enjoy for lunch, particularly on Saturdays when most great restaurants in Paris are closed. A dinner reservation here may be the most difficult to obtain in Paris unless you are French or a regular. The curried langoustines served with a sesame tuile is one of its signature dishes and also one of our favorites. The pigeon and lamb main courses served with satisfying reduction sauces and the freshest vegetables available are always quite memorable. On all five of our visits to this comfortable setting with elegant wall-length tapestries, we have found the service to be friendly and the staff quite approachable. The well-selected wine list includes some reasonably priced Burgundies from good vintages. This is classical French cooking at its best, which is why it is so beloved by Parisians and a destination so deserving of its three stars.

Pacaud's food often reflects changes in the seasons and above all respects the classical traditions of French cooking by seeking perfection in the way foods are presented. A three-star rating since 1986 has been achieved by trying to offer diners a transcendental experience they will never forget. His delicious, flavorful food has provided great memories for us on every visit.

Alain Passard

Our second visit to L'Arpège in 1996 was only two days after it was awarded its third star. The truffled cream and foie gras ravioli was particularly delicious. On our next visit in 1997 with our sons, we enjoyed an exceptional lobster salad in rice paper and a turbot in parsley sauce. When chef Alain Passard then decided to go primarily vegetarian in his main courses in 2001 (to demonstrate how creative he could be with these more challenging foods), we decided to stay away for a while.

When we finally returned for our fourth visit in October 2007, we knew that more fish and meat had returned to the menu. Some of the L'Arpège signature dishes were still there, including the tomato gazpacho soup with mustard ice cream and a twelve-flavored tomato served for dessert with Flowers of the Garden ice cream. There was a sense among all of us during this last meal, however, that some of the new cutting-edge creative courses we had enjoyed so much in the past were no longer being added to the menu. L'Arpège seemed to have become more concerned with turning tables and offering a formulaic menu of long-time favorites to handle the growing influx of tourists. And the prices may be the highest in Paris.

This son of musicians began cooking at age fourteen in his native Brittany and became a Michelin two-star chef by age twenty-six. His primary mentor was Alan Senderens, and he purchased Senderen's three-star Paris restaurant L'Archestrate in 1986 and renamed it L'Arpège. Passard's focus on vegetables was not surprising since they had always been his passion. So he saw this high-risk adventure of dramatically moving away from an emphasis on meat as a natural extension of something he had long wanted to do. And once he had earned his third Michelin star, Passard had the platform to make this change with the appropriate visibility.

Yannick Alleno

A bias against restaurants located in the major Paris hotels may finally have been overcome with the awarding of three stars in 2007 to Yannick Alleno at Le Meurice Hotel on the Rue de Rivoli. In a spectacular room inspired by the chateau at Versailles, Alleno puts his own innovations on classical French cooking. On our second visit in April 2007, we were particularly struck by Alleno's creativity in dishes such as the sea bass in a green garlic leaf and pea puree, and one of the best veal dishes we have ever had, served with a simple morel sauce and pasta. Our meal in 2010 included a particularly delicious partridge with salsify, and beef served with seaweed jam. Alleno was chef de partie at Le Meurice for a time in the 1990s before returning in 2003. He earned his third star in 2007 at the age of forty. His dishes can best be described as subtly eccentric with some Japanese influences. Alleno is concerned with the aesthetics of a dish so he does not put too many things on a plate or lose the essential purpose of the offering.

Frédéric Anton

Le Pré Catalen in the Bois de Boulogne west of the city offers a beautiful park setting for another of Paris' most recent three-star restaurants. On our second visit in October 2007, we enjoyed sea urchin and scallops done three ways, a creative tempura-style langoustine in a celery foam served with a seafood sauce, and a perfect rack of lamb with black trumpeter mushrooms. The tasting menu is highly encouraged (to handle the increasing number of tourists), and chef Frédéric Anton continues to get highly positive word-of-mouth support for his cooking. On our initial visit in 2002, the restaurant was populated more by local Parisians. The à la carte offerings then included a memorable, delicious rare pigeon breast in broth served on broccoli shaved couscous with merguez sausage and chickpeas. The first meal, while Anton was striving to achieve his third star, seemed more exciting and authentically cutting edge.

After cooking at Boyer les Crayères, Anton served as chef de cuisine for the great Robuchon from 1989 to 1996. He came to Pré Catalen in 1997, earned two stars in 1999 and was awarded his third star in 2007. To achieve simplicity and a harmony of flavors in his cooking, he tries not to put more than five ingredients on a plate.

Guy Savoy

Guy Savoy has ridden his wonderful signature artichoke soup with black truffles and Parmesan shavings to a third star and expanded his culinary empire to include a Michelin two-star restaurant in Las Vegas. While we found his food in both locations to be of high quality and understand he remains a favorite of such well-respected food writers as Patricia Wells, it does not appear he is trying to break as much new ground with his menus as several of the other three-star chefs. The cold lobster with carrot cream in a lobster gelée accompanied by a lobster curry dressing was the other course we enjoyed the most on our only visit to the Paris location. Unfortunately, we were seated in an outer room where the service was less attentive and made the meal seem less special. The restaurant has an attractive modern decor of dark-paneled walls and leather seats.

Savoy earned three stars in 2002, which was seventeen years after earning his second star. He worked at Troisgros and in New York before moving to Paris in 1980. A native of Nevers in Burgundy, Savoy embraced the lighter nouvelle cuisine early in his career while always emphasizing luxury ingredients. Savoy tries to find ways to have fun with his cooking, and to offer a great experience to his many dedicated followers.

Christian Le Squer

Ledoyen is in a beautiful setting of nineteenth-century classical motifs on the second floor of a mansion in a park off the Champs Élysées near the Place de la Concorde. Chef Christian Le Squer earned his third star at a young age by offering classical dishes suitable for the setting with its elegant decor and wood paneling—clearly one of the most beautiful rooms in Paris. His turbot with a truffle cream sauce is one of the most decadent fish courses we have ever experienced. Diners feel pampered with the attentive, seamless service, but the deep wine list is quite aggressively priced. Our meals in 2002 and 2003 also included a delicious guinea hen with air-light pommes frites, and a pork tenderloin with crispy skin served with a blood sausage quenelle and gnocchi.

Le Squer came to Ledoyen in 1999 and earned three stars in 2002. This city-owned neo-classical pavilion was built in 1792 and is considered the oldest restaurant in Paris. Le Squer apprenticed at the Ritz Hotel restaurant, but his classical seafood orientation undoubtedly came from growing up on the coast of Brittany.

Eric Frechon

After years of striving, Eric Frechon at Hotel Le Bristol was finally elevated to three-star status in 2009. He has been the favorite chef of French President Nicolas Sarkozy, who undoubtedly appreciates the fact that the restaurant is only a few blocks away from the presidential palace. The beautiful wood-paneled room provides a comfortable and traditional setting for a refined dinner with flawless service and Frechon's creative cooking. The diced langoustines wrapped in cabbage with cinnamon and foie gras foam on top were flavorful and certainly unique. The rabbit course was cooked tandoori style, served on a pea puree, and accompanied by a delicious sausage of smoked octopus. The "Hen Egg" appetizer combined a broken egg yolk with spaghetti, morels, and green asparagus in a memorable veal and morel sauce and Comté cheese foam.

Frechon cooked at Taillevent, La Tour d'Argent, and the Ambassadors in the Hotel de Crillon before returning to the Hotel Le Bristol in 1999 after an eighteen-year absence. He received the French Legion of Honor in 2008 for his culinary contributions. Located on a prestigious Avenue Faubourg Saint-Honoré address, Le Bristol offers food that can be described as accessible, rustic, and provincial in its style.

Former Paris Three-Star Chefs

Nothing short of a sea of change has occurred in the three-star Michelin Guide scene in Paris over the last few years. The gastronomic temple that was Taillevent lost its third star in 2007 in one of the biggest shocks in recent years (it also lost its beloved owner Jean Claude Vrinat at about the same time). We had enjoyed some wonderful meals during our four visits there from 1990 to 2006. Sue's sixtieth-birthday dinner on our last visit included a creative lobster pudding with tarragon in a star anise emulsion, and a Pyrenees lamb in pimento sauce.

The hotel restaurant George V earned its third star only after it acquired chef Phillipe Legendre from Taillevant in 2003. Our 2004 meal in this breathtakingly beautiful room with spectacular flower displays was not at the level of cooking we had experienced with him at Taillvent previously. It was interesting to see food writer Patricia Wells hosting a table for six in the corner that night, and the staff was never distracted from serving the other diners. Le Cinq lost its third star in 2007, and Legendre then quit in April 2008.

Alain Senderens of Lucas Carton (where Sue had her fiftieth-birthday dinner) voluntarily gave up his three stars in 2006 to focus on more basic cooking (he has since earned back two stars). We had a delicious lunch there in 2009 that included almond-crusted langoustines and a soft pullet egg with a chanterelle and cockle emulsion in curry sauce.

Guy Martin of Grand Vefour losing his third star in 2008 is probably the hardest of all to understand. In a spectacular setting with two truly elegant and historic rooms overlooking the grounds of the Petit Palace, Martin cooks classical dishes such as a lobster tail served with green spaghetti and a lobster salad served in a pastry tower with green asparagus foam. His loyal cadre that has been running the front of the house for many years is both friendly and helpful and understands what great service means.

₮◎₮

CHAPTER 4
The Country French Three-Star Chefs

Jean-Georges Klein

In addition to three-star restaurants Michel Bras in Laguiole, Louis XV in Monaco, and Marc Veyrat on Lake Annecy (until 2010), the other thirteen current three-star country French restaurants offer a wide variety of regional foods and cooking styles. Several are in very remote country locations. L'Arnsbourg, sixty miles north of Strasbourg, is run by a brother/sister team, Jean-Georges and Cathy Klein. They have recently constructed a small hotel at the site (now managed by Jean-Georges' wife), but when we first visited in 2003, overnight diners were relegated to a very modest hotel five miles away. At what could have passed for a youth hostel for sixty euros per night (or sixty-five euros for the "suite" that contained two bunk beds), it was whimsical to see all the Mercedes and BMWs in the parking lot outside.

L'Arnsbourg features a beautiful dining room of understated elegance highlighted by large windows looking out on the heavily wooded countryside. The thoughtful Asian influences in the bar area set the mood for an evening of wonderful experiences. The remoteness of this setting—truly in the middle of nowhere (not even a town)—makes the quality of food and flawless service seem even more dramatic. Jean-Georges Klein's food contains none of the heaviness one might expect from being so close to the German border. Highlights of our first visit in 2003 included smoked eel with a translucent ravioli of pineapple and fennel with a shellfish sauce, a tagliatelle of chicken gelatin with caviar and lemon citron mousses, and a very creative emulsion of potatoes with thin crepes, chives, and pine nuts on top.

On our second visit in October 2009, we enjoyed a delicious meal that included an egg cooked at sixty-two degrees with chicory; a truffle emulsion with whipped potatoes; a trio of langoustines served as Carpaccio, broiled tails, and between a small kidney; baby frog legs with a tomato, coriander, parsley, and garlic sauce; and rack of lamb cooked in a salt crust with Parmesan risotto.

Klein succeeded his mother as executive chef in 1988, after never having taken a formal cooking class. The restaurant had originally been a hostel for coal workers and lumberjacks and can seem almost enchanted in its isolation. His unique dishes tell a story that can be described as witty, precise, and surprising because of the unexpected combinations of ingredients that somehow he can make seem harmonious.

Marc Haeberlin

South of Strasbourg on the peaceful Ill River is L'Auberge de l'Ill. This tribute to Alsatian cuisine has been provided by the two Haeberlin brothers who both worked well into their eighties to continue offering the best of the region's traditional dishes. On our first visit in 1994, we enjoyed the best cold goose foie gras we had ever tasted, served directly from a large crock with truffles and aspic; a fried skate with sesame seeds; a large langoustine with oriental slaw; a lobster with veal head and barley; and a classic venison preparation with apples and wild mushrooms.

When we returned fifteen years later in October 2009, Marc (the son of one of the brothers) had taken over as chef and greeted us warmly as we came in. We had to try the cold goose foie gras again and enjoyed a creative trio of crayfish preparations served as a velouté, with a poached langoustine, and as a quenelle served dim sum style. After an amazing mousseline of frog legs served inside a custard the size of a tennis ball, we had a whole wild mallard duck served tableside with red cabbage and a fried corn soufflé.

The restaurant was founded more than a century ago by

Haeberlin's great-grandfather. The traditional dishes indigenous to the Alsace region are quite different from other areas of France and always include plenty of potatoes and truffles.

Jacques Lameloise

Jacques Lameloise earned back his third star in 2007 after a two-year demotion and this continues to be Burgundy's only true gourmet restaurant, located just south of Beaune in an old post house in the modest community of Chagny. This genuinely nice man ran a family-oriented restaurant-hotel, often hosting groups of visitors overnighting on barges at the nearby canal in his private dining room. His wine list is chock-full of great Burgundy selections. In our first four visits there, we marveled at such dishes as lobster cream in gelée (1994); lamb in parsley crust (2000); a perfect roast pigeon in an elegant pigeon reduction sauce (2002); and salmon cooked four ways, including a mousse with crème fraîche (2003).

Lameloise originally earned three stars in 1979, after he became the third generation to run the restaurant in 1970. In 2009, Lameloise retired at age sixty-two and handed over what is now called Maison Lameloise to his nephew Eric Pras, who has cooked with Troisgros, Loiseau, Gagnaire, Westermann, and finally six years as the right-hand chef to Marcone.

In the fall of 2010, we invited the winemaker Jacques Seysses of Domaine Dujac and his wife Rosalind to join us at Lameloise for a special Sunday lunch. We shared several great wines, including the 2004 Lafon Meursault-Perrières and 2002 Roumier Bonnes-Mares. The food highlights included oysters en gelée with a green apple emulsion, hot foie gras wrapped in potato with a truffle bullion, and a Bresse chicken served two ways: the breast with Swiss chard and hazelnuts and the leg confit served under creamy whipped potatoes. The sweetbreads and pigeon courses were also creatively prepared.

Jean-Michel Lorain

Côte Saint Jacques in Joigny, north of Burgundy, has gone through the transition from father to son Jean-Michel Lorain, and the restaurant has moved across the road to be on the River Yonne. The new entrance is a spectacular upgrade over its modest predecessor. After losing a star briefly during the move, it has been a solid three-star destination again since 2004, with a thoughtful menu and interesting wine list. Among our five visits beginning in 1992, we have enjoyed perhaps the greatest lamb course of our lives in 1997, which was a tiny rack of Pyrenees lamb almost white in color and perfectly cooked. The sweetness of the meat made a lasting impression on all of us. Other memorable courses have included bar (sea bass) in crab sauce with squid-stuffed eggplant (1995), and lobster tail on fennel puree with Asian spices (2002).

Jean-Michel helped earn the restaurant's original third star with his father in 1986, and in 1993 was named Chef of the Year by Gault Millau. He interned at Troisgros, Taillevant, and with the Swiss master chef Fredy Girardet. His eclectic and creative dishes reflect thoughtful ideas from all over France—not just his Burgundy region.

Michel Troisgros

The greater Lyon area boasts four three-star restaurants. Troisgros, northwest of Lyon in the industrial city of Roanne, has also transitioned from a legendary uncle and father to son Michel, who is a wonderful host and loves traveling the world. Over our first four visits, we noticed that his à la carte menu contained several of his outstanding specialties such as lobster and lamb, while his tasting menus always featured some very creative selections. His thoughtful wine list at amazingly reasonable prices matches the high quality of his food. This is a destination restaurant for serious foodies, and the generously sized rooms overlook an inside courtyard with a garden.

Our favorite courses have included crayfish on yellow pomegranate sauce (2003); shrimp with bread crumbs and garlic (2005); and a perfectly grilled lobster with herb butter (2006). We invited the Burgundy winemaker Alex Gambal and his wife Diana to join us on our fifth visit in October 2009. We brought wines for Michel Troisgros, who reciprocated with a special chestnut soup as a starter. Everything that came out of the kitchen that evening was perfect, including baby frog legs with cauliflower, rouget with pimento sauce, poached turbot, and small veal kidneys. We had many memorable wines that evening including three from the 1996 vintage: Domaine Leflaive Puligny-Montrachet Clavoillon, Domaine Dujac Clos de la Roche, and Bruno Clair Gevrey Chambertin, all preceded by a 2002 Coche-Dury Puligny-Montrachet Les Enseignères.

Troisgros is increasingly becoming one of our favorite restaurants in France. Our visits in 2010 and 2011 offered evidence of increasing Asian influences in a crayfish à la nage and a beautiful mosaic of vegetable squares. And in contrast, we were treated to a classic lobster in a lobster bisque cream sauce, and a stunning blackened rack of lamb. The spring 2011 menu included three large white asparagus spears in dramatic mustard, basil and truffle wraps, and an unusual rabbit roulade stuffed with langoustines. Michel's son Cesar has returned from a year staging at the French Laundry in Napa Valley to join him in the kitchen.

Michel's father and uncle originally joined his grandfather as chefs and earned two stars in 1965 and three stars in 1968. The restaurant has been at the current location across from the main train station in Roanne since 1930. Michel came to Troisgros in 1984, and is influenced by his Italian grandmother's cooking (evidenced in his love for tomatoes and use of seasonal citrus fruits), as well as his twice a year trips to Japan. He embraces acidity in his cooking and continues to develop sophisticated but uncomplicated dishes that bridge traditional and new cooking techniques.

Georges Blanc

Northeast of Lyon is Georges Blanc, whose family restaurant has cooked some of the most delicious Bresse chicken in France for several generations. While Blanc has grown much more commercial over the years by opening a large gourmet store, gift shop, and a bistro in his flower-bedecked hometown of Vonnas, he delivers classic comfort food as well as anyone. We have now had seven visits to enjoy his special baby frog legs cooked in garlic and butter, and the Bresse chicken either in a creamed foie gras or morel sauce. Selections from an impressive and reasonably priced Burgundy wine list have complemented all our meals there, including several bottles of the rare Madame Ferret Pouilly Fuisse produced by this now deceased special lady.

Because of the amount of butter and cream found in almost every dish, not everyone who visits what is acknowledged to be the largest three-star restaurant in France is enamored with the healthfulness of the food. Georges Blanc took over from his mother in 1968 at age twenty-five and earned his third star in 1981. The fifth generation is now cooking at this family inn that was founded in 1872 and was known as La Mère Blanc at one time. Now approaching seventy, Blanc has certainly been the genius primarily responsible for developing such a winning formula for commercial success.

Régis Marcon

Southwest of Lyon in the remote town of Saint Bonnet le Froid, are Régis Marcon and his son Jacques; their panoramic new restaurant is a relaxing hillside retreat. While not highly sophisticated food, the flavors are quite intense and satisfying. A great deal of creative thought goes into the multiple amuses that often include liquid surprises in shot glasses. Marcon is a highly dedicated chef who prides himself on having passion about everything he does. His breakfasts, which can include omelets with truffles, are especially delicious and satisfying. During our two dinners there in 2000 and 2002 (when it was called Auberge et Clos des Cimes), we particularly remember his pigeon with hazelnuts, venison with dried blueberries, and almond-crusted foie gras with lentils, quinoa, and mushrooms.

Since opening the original restaurant in 1982, Marcon has bootstrapped his way to international recognition by winning the prestigious Bocuse d'Or competition in 1995 and earning a third Michelin star in 2005. He cooks almost exclusively with such local or regionally produced foods as mushrooms, lentils, cheese, beef, veal, and deer. He is another chef like Michel Bras who has been wildly successful in a remote home town.

Paul Bocuse

In the northern suburbs of Lyon resides the great ambassador of French cooking, Paul Bocuse, who is now in his mid-eighties. Unfortunately, this legendary chef has not developed the kitchen staff to maintain the same level of greatness he often provided in the 1970s and 1980s. Friends who have eaten there recently are shocked by how average the food has become. On our one visit in 1970, however, we will never forget an incredible loup de mer en croute, which was an entire fish covered with a pastry shell; it featured raised fish scales and a face on the crust. After beef tournedos and cheese, we left that meal as full as I have ever been in my life. I had to walk around for an hour before getting back in the car to drive to our nearby hotel, and don't recall ever breaking into such a sweat from eating.

Bocuse enthusiastically embraced the nouvelle cuisine of his era by emphasizing high-quality, fresh ingredients. He enjoyed great success early in his career by gaining three Michelin stars in the mid-1960s. Coming from a family of German chefs dating back to the 1600s, Bocuse has resisted changing the way he cooks and has continued to use a somewhat heavy hand with butters and sauces by today's standards.

Anne-Sophie Pic

On the way south from Lyon to Provence, a favorite destination for many is Pic in the modest town of Valence. The torch has been passed successfully from father to daughter Anne-Sophie who regained Pic's third star in 2007. One of the most spectacular upgrades we have ever seen in atmosphere and elegance for a restaurant and hotel transpired between our visits in 1993 and 2006. Not surprisingly, Anne-Sophie emphasizes fresh Provençal ingredients in her thoughtful menus. While none of the courses was uniquely memorable (because the flavors are more subtle and simple with hints of sweetness), the food is consistently delicious and satisfying. Her father's specialty was Bresse chicken cooked in a paper bag, and we also fondly remember an unusual lobster and pigeon salad with green beans in a walnut oil. Sophie's most interesting courses for us have included a peach-infused langoustine with anise powder served with pea puree, and a turbot with tarragon foam, rhubarb strips, and baby mussels.

Anne-Sophie is currently the only female three-star chef in France and the first since Lyon's Mere Brazier in 1933. She is also the first third-generation chef to earn a third star, following her grandfather André in 1934 and her father Jacques in 1973. Her dramatic return to the family business in 1992 after her father's death, and then taking over the kitchen in 1998 with little formal training has made her achievement seem even more dramatic. A shy but determined individual, Anne-Sophie's food reflects her high standards and desire for excellence in all she produces.

Michel Guérard

For years, the greatest chef in Southwest France has been Michel Guérard. His three-star restaurant in Eugénie les Bains is integrated into a world-class spa inside a large gated estate. Hotel guests can choose among several different buildings for their stay, including the original convent that has been furnished by Madame Guérard with eye-catching antiques. Complementing the famous minceur (minimalist) cooking (using vegetable sauces instead of butter, cream, and flour) that Guérard pioneered to great acclaim in the 1990s, is a thoughtful menu of locally produced meats and vegetables to be enjoyed in an elegant country dining room. During our three visits (1992, 2001, and 2008), we have watched his gourmet menu continue to evolve to bolder flavors. The recent tasting menu, which was our most satisfying meal, included a cold asparagus soup with morels and a floating island of egg whites, and lobster grilled in a wood-burning oven with butter sauce and a carrot and ginger puree.

Guérard began his career at Maxim's in Paris and opened his own restaurant, Pot-au-Feu, there in 1965. He had earned two stars by 1971 before moving to Eugénie les Bains in 1974 to develop a restaurant as part of his wife's spa. In 1977, he earned his third star while applying his wonderful culinary techniques to achieve simple flavors using the highest quality ingredients. Now in his late seventies, Guérard currently has two head chefs executing his thoughtful menus and has been an effective mentor over the years to a large number of other three-star chefs currently cooking in France.

Gerald Passédat

One of the most recent three-star elevations in France is Le Petit Nice, located on the water in the gritty Mediterranean port city of Marseilles. After surviving many wrong turns and the narrowest street we have ever driven down to reach a hotel, we enjoyed both a lunch and dinner of outstanding seafood and bouillabaisse. The Passédat family has owned this restaurant for several generations. Finally receiving its third star in 2008 was special to everyone including the patriarch Jean Paul, who still is there to greet the guests after retiring many years ago as head chef.

Supported by a great white wine list and featuring a bright, comfortable dining room with a pleasant view of the harbor and the Mediterranean sea, Gerald Passédat offers such creative courses as a hot crab salad with roe and a ten-pepper sauce; anemones served in both milk foam with caviar and also deep fried in a crispy pastry chip; and lobster wrapped in red and white cabbage with ginger-infused blue flower broth. The bouillabaisse tasting menu included both lobster and sea bass in a saffron sauce, and a local white fish in a classic fish soup. Service was particularly thoughtful and welcoming.

Passédat's grandfather Germaine originally purchased the property in 1917, and his father Jean Paul earned two stars by 1981. Gerald cooked at the Bristol and Hotel de Crillon and with Troisgros and Michel Guérard before returning to Marsailles in 1984 and taking over the kitchen in 1990. He soon realized the sea would be his vegetable garden, and he could offer diners the purest flavors of freshly caught fish. Using techniques that were developed for cooking meat by one of his mentors, Jean Troisgros, Passédat produces memorable food that he pairs with fresh herbs and vegetables from Provence.

Gilles Goujon

The newest Michelin three-star restaurant in France (awarded in 2010) is Auberge Du Vieux Puits in the remote country village of Fontjoncuse near the Mediterranean coastal city of Narbonne. Our fall 2011 visit with Chef Gilles Goujon met all expectations for three-star food, with his signature dish, a reconstructed egg filled with a truffle sabayon sauce and sliced black truffles on top, and a delicious mushroom cappuccino on the side. All the courses were thoughtful and creative, and Goujon did an especially good job on the main courses: pigeon breast with pistachio crust and a large slice of duck breast with a violet sauce, accompanied by a whimsical presentation of wild mushrooms served in a porcelain duck foot dish. The flavorful desserts included an orange flower ice cream under a meltable fig sheet, and a chocolate biscuit with vanilla cream and fresh wild strawberries.

Cooking at Béziers beginning in 1977 and later at Moulin de Mougins, Goujon moved to this small village of Fontjoncuse in 1992. Earning his first star in 1997, his second in 2001, and chef of the year honors in 2010, he cooks from the heart with an inventive spirit, while respecting traditional cuisine and reflecting seasonal produce on his menus.

La Côte D'Or (now Le Relais Bernard Loiseau)

The final current three-star restaurant we have visited in France is the saddest story of all. No chef has ever aspired to a third star more than Bernard Loiseau of La Côte D'Or in Saulieu. When he finally achieved this goal in 1991, he wrote a book about how he had literally willed himself to do anything necessary to earn this great honor. When rumors were rampant about the possibly of him losing his third Michelin star in 2003, and the Gault Millau guide dramatically lowered his rating from nineteen to seventeen, he committed suicide. Whereas we have enjoyed several memorable meals there over the years, the current restaurant being managed by his widow and his long-time sous chef Patrick Bertron may not be at its former level of greatness. Our first great meal in France in 1970 was here at La Côte D'Or, two years before Loiseau came to the kitchen. I will never forget the perfectly roasted chicken with truffles under the skin and the incredible bottle of 1961 Le Montrachet from Bouchard Père that accompanied it. Our 1990 visit included a memorable langoustine course in a delicate seafood sauce. By 1997, Loiseau was at the peak of his culinary talents. He prided himself on using a minimum of flour, cream, or spice in order to emphasize the natural flavors of the ingredients. His traditional baby frog legs to be dipped in concentric circles of pureed garlic and parsley were dazzling, and the perch in a red wine reduction sauce was equally memorable. When we ordered these same two courses upon our return in 2000, however, the quality of the ingredients had slipped, and the sauces even separated on the plate. We decided at the time that there was no reason to ever return. The Michelin Guide, to date, has been hesitant to lower its three-star rating.

⚟

CHAPTER 5

Other Noteworthy French Chefs

IT SEEMS APPROPRIATE TO COMMENT ON SEVERAL OTHER recently demoted three-star restaurants that offered some of our fondest memories at the time. What is particularly unfortunate has been the decline of Les Crayères in Reims following the retirement of the charismatic Gerard Boyer. Once rated by *Travel and Leisure* magazine as the "top hotel and restaurant destination in the world," things changed rapidly when Boyer's sous chef of many years took over as head chef and quickly lost the third star. Les Crayères panicked, fired him, and has never completely recovered.

This idyllic setting on an eighty-acre walled estate in the heart of the Champagne estates features sumptuous rooms and two elegant adjoining dining rooms. Vintage champagnes at retail prices flow like water. Boyer's decadent signature courses included a whole black truffle in crust with a Périgord truffle sauce, a Maurice salad featuring cubes of lobster and foie gras, with haricot vert (green beans) and black truffles tossed in a delicious vinaigrette. We experienced many great memories (including birthday dinners) during our seven visits there over the years.

At Les Loges de l'Aubergade in the hilltop village of Puymirol, Michel Trama earned his third star in 2004 but lost it in 2011. The well-appointed rooms are comfortable and the elegant stone walls and arches of the restaurant provide a setting reminiscent of dining in the Middle Ages. The deconstructed ratatouille appetizer on our second visit in 2005 was a particularly creative course, with spicy tomato and yellow pepper sorbets served with onion and eggplant compotes. The deconstructed salt cod foam balls with potato tuiles were whimsical as well as delicious. A roast pigeon was served with lemongrass, beets, and a beetroot leaf.

Antoine Westermann earned three stars at his Buerehiesel Restaurant in Strasbourg in 1993, then gave them all up in 2007 when he passed the head chef responsibilities to his son Eric (who earned his first star in 2008). In this bucolic setting in the l'Orangerie public park in the middle of the city, we enjoyed wonderful meals in 1994 and 2003 when Westermann was in his prime. This humble, self-effacing man, with particularly creative sauces for his fish and game courses, cooked a number of memorable courses for us including a venison and foie gras terrine with wild chanterelles and celery root; lobster in saffron sauce with parsley risotto; wild duck in blood sauce with a duck sausage stuffed potato (1994); frog legs in chervil sauce; poached duck foie gras in duck consommé; and roasted venison leg with red wine sauce and fresh fig (2003). His bistro, Mon Vieil Ami, on the Île Saint Louis in Paris, has been a real success since its opening in 2003, and offers modern Alsatian cuisine at reasonable prices.

Marc Meneau at L'Espérance in Vezelay lost his third star in 1999, regained it in 2004, and lost it again in 2008; he has struggled to avoid bankruptcy in recent years. Our five visits between 1990 and 2004 included some especially wonderful dining memories. A simple lunch in 1990 approached perfection, and included fresh oysters in an oyster gelée with crème fraîche, as well as some wonderful fresh green asparagus in a vinaigrette. Our second meal in 1993 was "other worldly," and at the time I considered it to be the best meal of my life (the Robuchon meal in Paris did not come until 1996) because of the satisfying flavors of each course. It featured such classic but obviously labor-intensive dishes as lobster crème in gelée, an onion and foie gras tart with an onion cream sauce, and a perfectly cooked rare pigeon in a delicious pigeon reduction sauce with mushrooms and green beans.

Our most recent meal in 2004 (after Meneau had regained his third star for a brief time) was good but seemed much less innovative. I felt that the standard fare he served of foie gras, lobster, and lamb were satisfying but the preparations were nothing special or innovative compared to what other three-star restaurants in France were doing. L'Espérance is in a beautiful country setting in a town with a legendary cathedral, so Vezelay is always worth the visit.

Our first visit to Jardin de Sens in Montpellier in Southern France (on my birthday in October 1997) was an extraordinary meal of lobster in vanilla sauce with herb ravioli, duck foie gras with crepes and apples, and pigeon in crust with parsnip puree. The twin brother chefs, Jacques and Laurent Pourcel, earned their third star the following year. Our meal in 2000 was also quite good and included a langoustine mousse with a Cajun tuile, a cepe emulsion with a butternut-stuffed ravioli, and langoustines with a caramel sauce. Our next experience there in 2001 did not inspire the same kind of "wow" as prior visits, and the twins lost their third star in 2005 after expanding into Paris.

From 1933 when he received his third star until his death in 1955, the most important chef in the world was Fernand Point at La Pyramide in Vienne, south of Lyon. He trained a generation of chefs including Alaine Chapel, the elder Troisgros, and Bocuse, and was one of the first chefs to embrace the nouvelle cuisine movement, emphasizing freshness and featuring the products of the season. His current successor at La Pyramide (since 1989) Patrick Henriroux, is a dedicated chef worthy of his two stars who serves classical cuisine respecting the traditions of this great restaurant.

In our four meals at La Pyramide since 2002 (it is very convenient to the Lyon airport), we have enjoyed some outstanding courses including veal with roasted garlic in veal demi-glace; baby frog legs in parsley juice and pea puree; a mullet egg and spaghetti served with scallops in a cream sauce of green asparagus; a crab soufflé with caviar and parsley oil; and rack of lamb with sun-dried tomato au jus served with a potato pancake and leeks. The Rhône wine list, not surprisingly, is quite outstanding, since the Northern Rhône vineyards start not too far south of Vienne.

One of Point's most famous protégés was Alain Chapel who returned to the family bistro in Mionnay north of Lyon, gained his first star in 1967, and was awarded three stars in 1973. He was famous for such dishes as stuffed calves' ears with fried parsley, and a truffle-stuffed chicken cooked in chicken broth inside a pork bladder. Chapel had a major influence on a number of young chefs including Troisgros and Ducasse, who felt it a privilege to learn from this master. This intellectual, soft-spoken man stressed perfection in the rigor of his techniques, which emphasized preserving the integrity of high-quality ingredients so they would taste as natural as possible.

After Chapel passed away in 1990 at the young age of fifty-three, his longtime sous chef Phillipp Jousse and his widow Suzanne carried on many of his traditional dishes. The Michelin Guide removed a star upon his death (supposedly out of respect for this legendary chef), and the restaurant has never been able to earn its third star back, which has been a tremendous disappointment to all involved.

At our only meal there in October 1997, we felt a sense of history sitting in the historic dining room, drinking a legendary 1985 Ponsot Clos de la Roche from the excellent wine list (and tasting an amazing 1962 Comte de Vogue Musigny from an adjacent table). Among the memorable courses were shrimp and potato fritters in cream, scallops and potatoes with black truffles, a grouse served in crust, and duck breast with cèpes.

From World War II until he died at the age of ninety-three in 1990, Raymond Thuilier was regarded as one of the greatest chefs in the world. We managed to visit his Oustau de Baumanière restaurant in Les Baux-de-Provence in 1970 on our initial France trip. Because we could not afford to stay there, we were greeted rather coolly and did not receive the best attention or service in the restaurant that evening, despite ordering a DRC (Domaine de la Romanée-Conti) Grand Echezeaux and the full tasting menu.

For this reason, we did not return until 2000, despite the spectacular setting in a horseshoe-shaped canyon in the heart of the Alpilles mountains of Provence. At this time, Thuilier's grandson Jean-André Charial, who is a chef, was running the restaurant. We have now had nine dinners there, and love the ambiance of the stone arches in the dining room and the views while hiking along the spectacular bluffs above the town of Les Baux. Jean-André is a wonderful host and still draws from a noteworthy wine cellar built over the years to complement the delicious Provençal food. He has been frustrated that the restaurant has not been able to regain its third star, which was taken away in 1990. Jean-André recently hired Sylvestre Wahid, who apprenticed for ten years under Ducasse as his chef de cuisine, with the objective of persuading Michelin to finally upgrade its rating.

We have many great memories of the food at Oustau de Baumanière over the past decade, including a langoustine mousse with zucchini flowers, roast pigeon served between parsnip chips with a celery root puree, Pyrenees lamb with cheese scalloped potatoes, pork trotter with foie gras, green asparagus and morels in asparagus puree, langoustines with langoustine ravioli in a coriander and ginger broth, and a tomato-crusted pigeon.

The rapid decline of La Tour d'Argent from one of the jewels of Paris three-star restaurants in the 1970s to two stars in 1996, and finally to one star in 2006 was unfortunate but not surprising. Originally opened as an inn in 1582, with a spectacular view of Notre Dame Cathedral, it was for a long time the primary Paris destination for fashionable tourists and locals alike. The restaurant resisted all attempts to update its old-style cuisine, which featured a roasted pressed duck raised on its farm, with a numbered souvenir postcard for each. Despite outstanding service and a wine cellar that at one time totaled a half million bottles, La Tour d'Argent did not change as the food revolution passed it by.

We have our eyes on two chefs currently earning two stars who we believe have been more than worthy of a third star for

OTHER NOTEWORTHY FRENCH CHEFS

a number of years. Edouard Loubet at La Bastide de Capelongue in Bonnieux may be the best chef in the Luberon—and probably all of the Provence. His alfresco lunches are memorable, and he offers bold, satisfying flavors in uniquely creative presentations, with proper respect for the basics of classical cooking. We have followed the relocation of his primary restaurant from Lourmarin to Bonnieux and enjoyed six really great meals with him over the past decade. Our lunch in October 2008 was an eleven-course tasting menu made memorable by a hot and cold foie gras equivalent to what the great Veyrat achieves, a boudin blanc sausage made from pheasant, a fresh baby anchovy in almond milk, and sea bass in a sage cream sauce.

A 2011 dinner with Loubet was the highlight of our spring trip and included a number of memorable courses such as a cream of escargot soup with herbs of the Luberon, white asparagus and morels with licorice, sea bass in a sage broth, and a rack of lamb with burned thyme smoke served with decadent au gratin potatoes. A hot cedar soufflé with clove ice cream was a great finale.

An ex-member of the French alpine ski team and a poet, Loubet is married to Marc Veyrat's niece. He raises herbs, aromatic plants, and grasses in his own garden. Loubet seeks lightness in his cooking style while showing respect for the terroir. Open eight months a year, Loubet rotates through six highly creative menus each year that emphasize unique flavor combinations of organic ingredients.

The other two-star restaurant we have enjoyed greatly is Gill in the industrial Normandy city of Rouen. It is located in the shadow of the famous cathedral that Monet painted in different lights and seasons, and the food has continued to improve on each of our four visits. The wine list is particularly thoughtful and very reasonably priced. Everything on Gilles Tournadre's tasting menu is of the highest quality, and our most recent fall 2007 visit featured such courses as a perfectly cooked duck foie gras on a caramelized turnip, lobster on black risotto with a lobster sauce and purple basil, John Dory on artichoke puree with black truffle foam, and roasted pigeon presented in the legendary Rouennaise blood sauce, which is worth a visit by itself just to experience.

Tournadre began cooking at age fifteen and spent time at Taillevant and Lucas Carton to hone his techniques. He opened Gill in 1984 and had earned his first star by 1985 and his second in 1990. Tournadre is a very down-to-earth, private person whose wife Sylvie works the front of the house seamlessly to make everyone feel very welcome.

Chef Alexandre Bourdas of Sa Qua Na (Saveurs Qualité Nature) is also emerging as one of France's most important chefs of the next generation. After cooking with Michel Bras in Laguiole and then opening Bras' restaurant in Tokyo in 2001, he and his wife returned to the seaside village of Honfleur on the Normandy coast of France in 2005 to open this exciting new restaurant. Among the outstanding courses offered on his special Vert Olive tasting menu for our April 2009 meal were steamed codfish in fermented milk sauce with jasmine, chickpeas, baby oysters, and baby turnips; rare cooked Segala veal served cold with yogurt cream and candied Mexican lemon; hot duck foie gras with fromage blanc and beetroot sauce; and rare-roasted Anjou beef with coffee cream cauliflower puree, watercress, and hazelnuts. This has already become a Michelin two-star restaurant and is a particularly attractive draw for young people in the town. Bourdas also cooked with Michel Guérard and Régis Marcon before joining the Bras family.

On our spring 2011 trip with our friends Tom and Mary Raciatti, we returned to San Martin in Vence after a fifteen-year hiatus to sample the food of the new chef Yannick Franques. He has earned two Michelin stars in his first three years there. The meal certainly did not disappoint with several highly creative offerings including langoustines with black sesame seed and yuzu sauce; "Mystery of the Egg," a slow-cooked yolk with whipped egg white and brioche crumbles in a Parmesan sauce; and an herb-crusted lamb with zucchini ravioli stuffed with goat cheese in a black garlic sauce. The setting high above the Mediterranean offers spectacular views for miles around.

An alfresco lunch at the nearby Colombe d'Or in Saint Paul

de Vence is always uplifting and is one of the best settings anywhere for people-watching. The signature vegetable crudités can be followed by a memorable cream of broccoli and zucchini soup, then several tasty main courses of Provençal fare.

Two of the more memorable visits for sheer fun and comfort food in the Provence area have been to the one-star "Truffle King" Bruno Clement at Chez Bruno near Lorgues. Our first visit in April 2000 featured very generous portions of shaved truffles on top of all four courses: asparagus soup with truffle oil, fresh green asparagus and foie gras with Parmesan cheese in a truffle sauce, sliced potatoes in creamed truffle sauce, and duck breast with a truffle sauce and organ compote.

On our return visit two years later, the price of the prix fixe dinner with truffles had more than doubled, and the truffles shaved on top were much less generous. We enjoyed three courses of a truffle in crust with truffle sauce (like Boyer Les Crayères), shrimp with spring vegetables, and a filet of beef cooked rare. With fresh black truffles selling for 1,000 euros per kilo or more, this was still a special experience. French kings have proclaimed truffles to be a great aphrodisiac, and Bruno has never been hesitant to note that he loves "both truffles and women," and that this rare fungus is believed to result from the cross-fertilization of male and female spores.

The small hotel itself is really over the top, featuring the large Yellow Room bedroom that was obviously designed to pamper visiting chefs in a space large enough to hold a small convention. The front wall of the hotel facing the entrance from the road is painted to show Bruno as the Christ figure at the Last Supper, with legendary three-star chefs such as Ducasse and Bocuse among the twelve French chefs featured as his disciples.

᪶⚬᪶

CHAPTER 6

Switzerland's Incredible Three-Star Chefs

Philippe Rochat

Two of the great recent three-star restaurants in Switzerland are both French influenced. Since taking over the legendary Fredy Girardet's three-star restaurant in Crissier outside Lausanne in 1996, Philippe Rochat has been putting his own stamp on classical cooking. The setting offers comfortable, understated elegance and is the equal of many grand Paris restaurants. Among the memorable courses we enjoyed in 2006 on the eleven-course grand chef's menu were the classic cold pressed foie gras with a quince orange gelée layer and black quince seeds; turbot in consommé with Thai spices; wild hare cooked for four hours and served with an upside-down pyramid cone of celery coated phyllo; and a Scottish lobster in black radish cream sauce.

Rochat's food is delicious because he has always emphasized the quality of the ingredients. His reputation has been built on using no more than three flavors in any dish so as to let the course speak for itself. Rochat suffered a great personal tragedy when his wife Franziska (who was a marathon runner) died in an avalanche in 2002.

Gérard Rabaey

At Pont de Brent, high above the north shore of Lac Leman, Chef Gérard Rabaey delivered flavorful, creative offerings in a more informal setting. Among our favorites from his nine-course menu gourmand in 2006 were the savarin of frog legs in garlic custard with shaved black truffles and parsley puree, Breton lobster in a saffron bouillabaisse sauce with white beans and cabbage, and a citron soufflé with citron and coconut ice creams. The brilliant New York City chef Daniel Humm of Eleven Madison Park (which recently received the special four-star *New York Times* rating and three Michelin stars) obtained much of his early training under Rabaey. Rabaey was raised in Normandy (Caen), began cooking at fifteen, and opened Pont de Brent in 1980. He earned his third star in 1998 and recently turned the restaurant over to Stéphane Decotterd who now has a two-star rating.

YI©If

CHAPTER 7
Spain—Leading the Food Revolution?

SPAIN'S EMERGENCE AS A MAJOR CULINARY DESTINATION HAS been dramatic over the past decade, and the country's food has taken its place among the cutting-edge cuisines of the world. Before Ferran Adrià's generational transformations at elBulli, San Sebastián in the northwest corner of Spain had firmly established itself as the food capital of Spain. Barcelona and Madrid have been trying to play catch-up ever since.

The Spanish are passionate about their food (and their dining hours, which are the latest in Europe). Tapas (small plates) have long been the staple of casual eating in Spain, offering bites of attractively prepared fish, meat, and vegetables. San Sebastián has been a primary location for great tapas bars for many decades, with some of the best located in the old city. And when diners are through using their paper napkins, the custom is to throw them on the floor, which results in quite an accumulation by the end of an evening.

Juan Mari and Elena Arzak

Juan Mari Arzak, and now his daughter Elena, have been the pioneers in great Spanish cooking, as well as leaders in the transformation to more innovative cooking techniques. Their restaurant, Arzak, situated in a house built by his grandparents in 1897, was the first of the five current Spanish three-star restaurants to receive this recognition. The Arzaks are very proud of their role in helping lead the recent food revolution. Juan Mari has reached out to chefs throughout Spain to share his creative ideas and even collaborate on cookbooks. He has provided important stage opportunities for many aspiring chefs (it is not unusual to see thirty chefs with their white toques in the kitchen on any given night) to learn from a master.

Our first meal at Arzak in 1996 featured more simple, basic dishes such as the classic hake fish in a parsley sauce with olive oil. While we were at a tapas bar that evening, Elena and several girlfriends showed up and helped us order. It was fun to get to know her in a different setting and start a friendship that makes our trips to San Sebastián even more special. We brought the Arzaks copies of Charlie Trotter's basic and seafood cookbooks during our second and third visits because we thought they might not otherwise have easy access to English language books from the United States. We heard during our third visit that dinner might be delayed a bit since everyone in the kitchen was busy looking at the photographs in the seafood book. On Charlie Trotter's first visit, Elena brought out what was by then a dog-eared copy of one of his cookbooks to show him. When asked where she got the book, Elena told Trotter that the Macdonalds wanted to help her learn about this "cutting-edge US chef."

We watched the restaurant change dramatically over the next decade, evolving into one of the most innovative in all of Spain. Juan Mari and Elena work as seamlessly together as Juan Mari's father and grandmother did. Elena's superior English allows her to work the front of the house effectively, and she has assumed a primary role in designing new menus that offer the best of fresh ingredients available each evening. Elena shared an observation with us that is both obvious and particularly insightful: that the most difficult part of planning a course is often choosing the proper accompaniments to the main item on the plate.

Among our recent favorite courses at Arzak have been the crayfish with dried tapioca and squid with green pepper toast (1999); shrimp with dried red chile sauce (2001); fried calamari with squid ink and calamari tartare (2003); poached egg with squid ink and parsley, and poached egg with chorizo puree

(2005); and poached egg with crispy chicken "Chicken to Egg" covered with an egg yolk sheet, and pigeon with a "puzzle" of gogi berries (2008). Their wine cellar is one of the finest in all of Spain.

Elena prepared a special meal of her favorite courses during our September 2011 visit. This included a yucca crisp tower stuffed with foie gras and green tea and coffee flavors; lobster with a parsley puree, chorizo oil and Parmesan/sesame red cracker; and crab covered with an edible sheet of anise waves, accompanied by a cone of crab coral and vegetables. An aromatic lamb shoulder featured verbena and sheep's milk crisps. This was followed by a unique sponge cake with beetroot sauce and candied pistachios, and chocolate "marbles" with basil and pineapple ice creams.

Juan Mari earned his third star in 1989 and has been a leader in developing the new Basque cuisine, which combines evolutionary fusion ideas with respect for traditional Basque dishes. All his suppliers are within one hour of San Sebastián. Elena began working in the restaurant at age eleven during summer holidays, apprenticed at Le Gavroche in London, and with Troisgros, Ducasse, Adrià, and several others before returning home. The Arzaks have a laboratory in which to practice gelifications and spherifications as well as a special storeroom of 1,400 starches, spices, seasonings, and herbs gathered from culinary trips around the world. Elena is constantly experimenting with color, which she believes is an "extra flavor," and regularly uses vinaigrettes to paint the plate.

Pedro Subijana

The Arzaks are close friends of Ferran Adrià and also of Pedro Subijana, the chef of Akelaŕe, which offers a spectacular view high above the Atlantic Ocean several miles west of San Sebastián. Elena's wedding reception was at Pedro's restaurant. Pedro finally received his well-deserved third Michelin star in 2007. He offers variations on traditional Spanish dishes such as sea bass with percebes (barnacles) and olive oil pears, foie gras with cherries and mustard ice cream (2003); and egg ribbon with cauliflower cream, and squab with quince and hazelnuts (2005). In 2008, we each ordered one of the two brilliant seven-course tasting menus that included false risotto (beetroot skin over five vegetables chopped to look like rice); "Mallard in the Forest" featuring rare duck breast covered with almonds and mushrooms on bread crumbs darkened to look like soil; and baby pig cooked in juice of bacon and served with egg white meringue, tomato powder and ham emulsion.

Subijana has continued to get even more creative. During our most recent visit in September 2011, we again enjoyed both of his eight-course tasting menus preceded by a "toiletry" amuse of tomato gel and basil served from a soap dispenser pump, soft white cheese inside a cold cream jar with dried fish in an edible packet resembling bath salts, and a "mouthwash cocktail." The mind-bending courses included a "red pasta" car-paccio with Parmesan and mushrooms; red mullet served with a praline of its head and bones and jellied spirals of soy, parley and white garlic; crab cooked in its own juice with pasta made to look like rice grains; a contrast of flavors and textures com-bining razor clams, veal shank, and cauliflower mushrooms; slow-cooked squid in squid broth with black onions; turbot with a reconstructed turbot cheek and a turbot chip made from its skin, and a delicious crispy skin suckling pig in an Iberian ham sauce.

Subijana's unusual restaurant name is based on the word ake-larre, which means a coven (gathering) of witches. He opened the restaurant in 1974 and has embraced the new Basque cui-sine of his friend Juan Mari with a passion. Pedro prides him-self on also being a teacher and mentor to younger chefs, and remains very active in his menu design and cooking execution.

Martin Berasategui

In a suburb of San Sebastián, the city's other three-star chef, Martin Berasategui, provided a delicious meal on our first visit in 2001 that included squid broth with squid ravioli and white squid, prawns in aspic with lettuce cream, and roast pigeon with pig's ear and spinach. Upon our return in 2003, however, only two tables were occupied in the entire dining room on a week night, so Berasategui was apparently not drawing well from the local community. Most of the meal, including a napoleon of smoked eel with foie gras and green apples, was not as exciting this visit, but a sea bass in a saworts bouillon green sauce with sesame salad was quite delicious.

Berasategui took charge of his family's restaurant at age twenty following the death of his father. He moved to his current site in 1993 and became the fourth Spanish chef to earn three stars in 2001. There are French influences from his training with Ducasse in Monaco and Michel Guérard. He focuses on achieving natural flavors while also using olive oil, garlic, and wine liberally in his cooking.

Andoni Luis Aduriz

Just outside San Sebastián, one of the most innovative and risk-taking chefs in the world, Andoni Luis Aduriz, cooks with no boundaries at Mugaritz. This two-star Michelin chef is considered by many to be one of the greatest deconstructionist chefs in the world, and the restaurant was ranked in the top three in the world in the S. Pellegrino annual survey in 2011. Our first visit in 2005 was memorable, with a sea bass in saffron sauce and rockfish confit, and a beef cheek cooked for forty-five hours in a vegetable beef sauce. We found our return meal in 2008 to be a little more uneven, but enjoyed the ravioli of crab and spring peas in a bluefish consommé, sheep's milk curd seasoned with hay and toasted fern (not Sue's favorite), and Iberian pork tails served with pan-fried langoustines in a reduction sauce infused with Iberian ham.

Our third visit in 2011 was our favorite, as the eighteen-course tasting menu stretched our imaginations on the boundaries of how food can be presented. In a series of often whimsical offerings, we enjoyed a deconstructed Bloody Mary (a slow-cooked tomato to which we added vodka, olive oil, and liquid spices to taste); mozzarella in whey emulsion infused with smoked black tea; a fish and Iberian ham broth to which we added seeds and spices we crushed from a pestle in front of us; a faux cheese made of fresh milk and linen seeds with edible clay as the rind; beef tongue straws with garlic flowers and onion gel drops; a diced sweetbread and artichoke ragout with a creamy kuzu bread; gelatinous noodles made from pork belly skin in an antiki fish broth with crispy rice; a Basque chulada beef with a beef butter emulsion and rock salt; and a cheese and flax seed cookie with a whiskey parfait. Knowledgeable servers and sommeliers make all guests feel special with a "this is your home" attitude.

Mugaritz means "oak border" in the Basque language, referring to the large tree in front of this destination restaurant located on top of the Errenteria mountain range. Andoni opened the restaurant at age twenty-six in 1998 after cooking at Arzak, Akelaŕe, and elBulli, and serving as chef de cuisine for Berasategui. He believes in feeding the mind as well as the stomach, while bridging the gap between cook and chemist. Andoni has studied the chemical components of scents to be able to mix fragrances, and continues to explore ways to invent new textures.

The Grill Man of Axpe

Another unique foodie experience awaits the adventurous diner at the Michelin one-star Etxebarri outside San Sebastián in the remote town of Axpe. Victor Arguinzoniz has reached cult status as a legendary grill man. He even has been known to grill caviar, and on our visit in September 2011, we enjoyed four grilled specialties: giant red Palamós prawns, oysters (served with crème fraîche and smoked seaweed), tuna belly, and an incredible bone-in ribeye that brought our appreciation of rare beef to a new level.

We have heard that the special grilling technology he has developed allows him to grill both sides of a steak at the same time. His refined technique highlights the natural tastes of even delicate foods by using custom-made mesh pans and different woods for specific ingredients. The restaurant is so hard to find that some diners have to hire taxis to lead them to the proper location.

Santi Santamaria

Santi Santamaria at Raco de Can Fabes in Sant Celoni, east of Barcelona, provided us with four interesting meals between 1996 and 2004. His numerous small plates, which were served as appetizers during our early visits, were stunning. We were particularly fond of the prune stuffed with duck rillette; pork belly (completely white lard) with Osetra caviar and a potato olive oil emulsion; a baby rabbit chop; pigeon tartare with dried artichoke hearts; and a truffle ball stuffed with foie gras. On our final visit, we missed these small bites since Santamaria presented us with less labor-intensive offerings and featured more French-style foie gras, lobster, and beef courses—delicious but certainly not as unique.

During our visit in 2001, we got lost in the city trying to find the restaurant because of road construction and stopped to ask directions. Only upon entering the restaurant did we discover it was in fact Santamaria himself who told us to follow him to the restaurant, and then let us park our car in his garage. While in a cooking competition in a large amphitheater early in his career, this fiery personality was said to have argued vehemently with judges who questioned how he was preparing a course. Santamaria passed away in early 2011, but clearly earned his reputation as one of Spain's legendary chefs.

In 1994, Santamaria became the first Catalan chef ever to earn three stars. He was self-taught and prided himself on using fresh, local ingredients from the Mediterranean area. Santamaria had great respect for classical cuisine and was influenced by Chapel's philosophy that emphasized traditional flavors.

Madrid and Barcelona

The elBulli alum Paco Roncero's two-star La Terraza del Casino has become Madrid's most exciting restaurant. With its breathtaking rooftop location, La Terraza offers an exciting tasting menu that includes creative variations on traditional dishes such as tuna belly with tuna mayonnaise and tomato gelée, veal tendon with tarragon sauce, faux broad beans with clams in a green sauce, squid with chopped vegetables and snails, a codfish cube with pil pil (vegetables and garlic), and oxtail stuffed with mushrooms and foie gras.

For years, Jordi Vila has been deconstructing traditional Spanish dishes at his one-star restaurant Alkimia in Barcelona. During our three visits there, we have enjoyed his unusual combinations of tuna tartar with soy foam, trout roe in white bean soup, and cod tripe with blood sausage ravioli. His baby squid and onion was paired with a faux Romesco sauce made out of strawberries instead of red peppers, while the "Head and Paw" (sheep's head and pig trotter constructed into one solid cube) was served with samfaina, a mixture of tomatoes and onions.

¶◎¶

CHAPTER 8
Finding the Gems in Italy

Heinz Beck

FINDING THE BEST HIGH-END FOOD IN ITALY IS NOT ALWAYS AS straightforward as it is in France or Spain because of the country's focus on simplicity in the quality of its ingredients. Many of the current Michelin three-star restaurants are in remote locations or unlikely venues such as the Waldorf Astoria's Rome Cavalieri Hotel where German chef Heinz Beck presides over a kitchen of Italian chefs. His restaurant, La Pergola, on the top floor of the hotel, offers a spectacular view of Saint Peter's Basilica from its balcony.

Beck's menu comes as close to classical cooking perfection as any restaurant in Italy. In 2001, we enjoyed such dishes as duck terrine with chocolate basil ice cream, black ravioli with cuttlefish, and salt-crusted venison with truffle broth. Upon our return for Sue's birthday dinner in 2009 with our sons, we chose the tasting menu; it included the grilled oyster on pumpkin cream with parsley foam, the liquid-center ravioli made with carbonara sauce and served with bacon and zucchini, the red mullet cooked in a crispy phyllo crust with tomato and anchovy oil, the duck foie gras served in a consommé of porcini mushrooms, and a slow-roasted Spanish Iberico black pig shoulder.

Beck began cooking at age sixteen and has been at La Pergola since 1994, earning his third star in 2005. He produces about eighty new dishes per year with emphasis on tasty, healthy foods that reflect lighter cuisines and Mediterranean flavors. While putting German discipline (he was born in Bavaria) into interpreting the nuances of Italian cuisine, he tries to transmit emotions through the balance of aromas, flavors, and colors. He is inspired by famous painters (Mondrian, Matisse) and mountain landscapes. Beck takes pride in running a calm kitchen with very little noise, and insists that visiting chefs stay a minimum of six months to really learn the food.

The Gems of Rome

Some of Rome's most satisfying dishes are found in smaller restaurants such as the family-run Agata e Romeo (one star) and Piperno in the old Jewish ghetto; the latter features fried artichokes and excellent veal dishes. Casa Bleve serves a delicious cold antipasto lunch featuring one of the best beef tartares we have ever had (this was the *New York Times* food critic Frank Bruni's favorite restaurant when he was on assignment as a reporter in Rome). Emile Colliane is a small, unpretentious restaurant that makes some of the best homemade pasta in Rome.

Nadia Santini

Dal Pescatore east of Verona near Mantua (in a place so remote that the only road signs were for the restaurant) has several surprises on its Michelin three-star menu, not the least of which was horsemeat with polenta, which I enjoyed for my birthday lunch in 1998. Dal Pescatore also featured guinea hen with spinach ravioli and a salmon pâté with lobster and caviar. It is a very modest restaurant that seats only thirty and is a prime example of what a chef who cooks with real integrity can accomplish.

Santini was raised in a small village outside Venice, and after she and her husband honeymooned in France in 1973, they were inspired to abandon traditional careers to revive the Santini family restaurant opened in 1925 by Nadia's grandparents as a fisherman's hut near the river. Santini has great respect for tradition in her cooking, so diners will come to know the generous heart and life of her land. Considered by many as Italy's undisputed queen of the kitchen, Nadia has been recognized by French food critic Gilles Pudlowski as "perhaps the best chef in the world."

Massimi Liano Alajmo

Le Calandre in Rubano, west of Venice, offers dramatic modern decor in an otherwise mundane village. Now considered one of Italy's most cutting-edge restaurants (it had two stars when we visited in 1998, and got its third star in 2002), we were quite impressed by such offerings as the pumpkin and Gorgonzola flan, white truffle gnocci, poached egg with spinach in truffled cream sauce, and spaghetti with prosciutto, mushrooms, and marjoram. We particularly appreciated the Italian custom of receiving a souvenir painted plate (a chicken with a pacifier in its mouth) from the chef who achieved his third star at age 28. The master winemaker Gaja himself was doing a special wine dinner there that night, and we would have loved to stay if we had not had another exciting dining experience waiting for us in Venice.

Alajmo joined the family restaurant in 1993 and earned his second star at age twenty-two in 1996, working with his brother Ruffaele who runs the front of the house. As a teenager, Alajmo cooked with Marc Veyrat and Michel Guérard in France, and shortly thereafter began pushing the envelope in all his presentations. The chandeliers at the restaurant are whimsically made from two dried cods.

Florence-Cibrèo and Enoteca Pinchiorri

We believe the most interesting restaurant in Florence is not the French-oriented, three-star Enoteca Pinchiorri, but rather Fabio Picchi's Cibrèo, which does not even have a star but is loved by the locals and serious foodies alike. In our five meals at Cibrèo over the years, we have particularly enjoyed the soups (tomato bread, porcini, yellow bell pepper, and potato with pork strips), the chicken gizzards and carrot stew, calamari with veal sausage and white beans, and the best crème caramel with caramel sauce I have ever tasted. In September 2010, we were able to sample a large number of tastes including a ricotta and Parmesan flan, tripe and veal in olive oil, several soups, a perfectly done vitello tonnato (veal in tuna sauce), eggplant Parmesan with three cheeses, veal meatballs stuffed with ricotta cheese, and cheesecake with orange marmalade.

This was in contrast to the meal we had the previous evening at Enoteca Pinchiorri. For years, we had resisted visiting this restaurant because we had heard it was trying to be more French than Italian. A wonderful Italy trip with our friends Sam and Marsha Dodson offered the opportunity to finally experience Florence's most visible restaurant, which has had three stars since 2004. Unfortunately, we really never got in synch with the wait staff, who tried to rush our orders. I really struggled with an overpriced wine list as I tried to find a special white and red of reasonable value and vintage. We found Annie Feolde's food (she is French) to be straightforward fare of lobster, pork, and veal. None of the courses were as creative or imaginative as might have been expected. We were left with an enormous bill and nothing special about the evening to recall. We did check this off our list of three-star restaurants to visit, and returning again is not likely.

Feolde's parents cooked at the Hotel Negresco in Nice where she grew up. She is self-taught and started cooking in order to provide small bites for her husband's bar in Tuscany. In 1972, they opened the Enoteca in Florence and earned three stars for the first time in 1992, before being demoted to two stars between 1994 and 2004.

David Scabin

Combal.Zero, a phenomenal one-star restaurant in the suburbs west of Turin, does not fit easily into any existing category of restaurant. In a stunning, ultra-modern setting next to a museum, chef Davide Scabin offers whimsical, unexpectedly delicious variations on a journey that combines traditional gourmet and peasant Italian cooking. It is not surprising that this restaurant is regularly included in most Top 50 lists in the world. Among our favorites of the sixteen-course tasting menu in 2005 were the virtual oyster composed of watermelon, almond, and dried tuna; the "Hambook" of prosciutto ham with melon gelée served inside clay that had to be shattered with a hammer; the "Harry Potter," which included oxtails, tripe, jelly apple, and red fruit risotto inside a candy wrapper; and the caramelized guinea hen with eucalyptus. Scabin's recommendation to drink champagne throughout the meal was appropriate (and continued after the meal in his kitchen until 2:00 A.M.). The dessert required inhaling a helium balloon and talking in high-pitched voices before eating the cherry inside a plastic ball.

Massimo Bottura

One of the great deconstructed food dining experiences will always be our September 2010 lunch at Osteria Francescana in Modena, which continues to surge toward the top of S. Pellegrino World's 50 Best Restaurants (#4 in 2011), while also earning three well-deserved Michelin stars for 2012. Cooking in this modest restaurant on a side street, Chef Massimo Bottura offers a number of signature dishes that make even the most serious foodies eager to see what will come next. Several of the other diners appeared to be chefs eating by themselves.

Our meal included a 1999 Voerzio La Serra Barolo—only a few days after our special visit with Roberto Voerzio in the Piedmont. A deconstructed mortadella was whipped without the fat and served with a garlic and pesto paste. The traditional culatello salami was accompanied by candied mustard and a three-year-old pancetta heavy with delicious fat. The ice cream bar on a stick was made of frozen foie gras that had been marinated in Calvados with aged balsamic and was coated with salty and bitter nuts.

The unforgettable next course featured different ages of Parmigiano-Reggiano cheese served as five interesting textures and tastes on one plate: twenty-four months as a cream on the bottom, thirty months as a soufflé, thirty-six months as a foam, forty months as a galette chip, and fifty months as frozen air. A ravioli of red lentils was accompanied by a cotechino sausage with a brown bean cream. The tortellini that followed was cooked in chicken broth and served with cream of Parmesan cheese. The final course was special short ribs from mountain black pigs marinated in balsamic and served with truffles and turnip puree. A spoon of 1941 (my birth year) rare balsamic vinegar made locally by the chef's family ended a spectacular eating experience.

Bottura cooked with Ducasse and Adrià before opening his restaurant in 1995 and earning his second star in 2005. Bottura is certainly in the center of the food revolution, and his ongoing research lets him be both a chef and artist interested in fusing concepts and foodstuffs. The passion he demonstrated in offering so many different flavors on a plate made this an unforgettable meal.

⅋◎⅋

CHAPTER 9

England—Beyond Steak and Kidney Pie

DESPITE AN UNFORTUNATE REPUTATION FOR UNEXCITING food, over the past two decades England has offered a number of interesting restaurant choices for serious gourmets. Our early experiences with the great London restaurants such as Albert Roux's Le Gavroche when it had three stars in 1986 (Sue's 40th birthday lunch), Marco Pierre White's exciting menus, and La Tante Claire under the brilliant Pierre Koffmann (later owned by Gordon Ramsay at the same location on Royal Hospital Road in Chelsea), were as good as most French restaurants at the time.

Heston Blumenthal

The English chef with the biggest influence on global cooking is now Heston Blumenthal at Fat Duck in Bray west of London. This molecular gastronomist may have more fun than any chef in the world while concocting his nitro-scrambled bacon and eggs ice cream, or his snail porridge made with braised snails, duck, ham, oats, and parsley butter. Upon arrival, diners are treated to a tea ball frozen with liquid nitrogen that, after being ingested in one bite, discharges smoke through the nose. (This dish was widely copied by many chefs, including Ferran Adrià, who paid proper tribute to Blumenthal.)

We noticed an increasing sophistication in Blumenthal's deconstructionist cooking between our two visits in 2004 and 2007. Among our other favorite courses were mustard ice cream with red cabbage gazpacho; sardine on toast ice cream with red caviar, lasagna of langoustine, pig's trotter and truffles; salmon poached in a licorice purse; rack of lamb with a puree of onion and thyme; and the Fat Duck "fountain" featuring a vanilla bean straw and pine sorbet powder. It was all good fun when he fooled us with gelées made from a orangish-colored beet and a blood-red orange that tasted the opposite of the traditional beet and orange flavors we thought we would be eating. We were told to eat the beet first, which we didn't, of course, by going for the dark red, orange-flavored gelée.

Blumenthal is self-taught in French classical techniques, and has had some valuable training under Marco Pierre White. A visit to Oustau de Baumanière in Provence at age sixteen changed his life forever when he fell in love with cooking. In 1995, Blumenthal bought a 450-year-old pub in Bray and began serving French bistro classics. By 2000, he was ready to offer a multi-course tasting menu reflecting his creative research, and amazingly he earned his third star as soon as 2004. Blumenthal became fascinated by the fact that diners would often taste his courses differently depending on what the dish was called. His appreciation for history even motivated him to try to reinterpret courses served at King James II's coronation in 1685, which included mock turtle soup and Beef Royal.

Gordon Ramsay

Born in Scotland, Ramsay studied under Marc Pierre White and Albert Roux when Le Gavoche was a three-star restaurant. He also spent three years in Paris with Guy Savoy and Jöel Robuchon before opening Aubergine back in London, at which he earned two stars.

Gordon Ramsay has grown into a global megastar with television shows and multiple restaurants after moving in 1998 from Aubergine to his Gordon Ramsay restaurant in Chelsea where he earned three stars in 2001. With restaurants now all over the world (in Versailles, Dubai, Prague, Tokyo, New York, and Los Angeles), this ex-rugby player is an effective self-promoter with his television shows and charismatic personality.

Our fondest memory was a dinner at the original Hospital

Road location in 2000 when he was still seriously focusing on cooking great food at this one restaurant. He dazzled us with such interesting courses as pumpkin soup with cèpes, sea scallops served with potatoes shaped like the scallops, tortellinis of lobster, and a pot-au-feu made with pigeon and foie gras. When Ramsay recently opened his first restaurant in France at the venerable Trianon Palace adjacent to Versailles, he was promptly awarded two Michelin stars.

Tom Aikens

One of my favorite local chefs in London has been Tom Aikens, who moved from Pied-à-Terre where he earned two stars at age twenty-six to open Tom Aikens in 2003 (which later had to close for a time because of financial difficulties). Among my favorite dishes from our two visits, in 2004 and 2007, were a foie gras with spices and dried fruit, turbot with artichoke puree in chervil sauce, pigeon with chestnut cannelloni and turnip fondant, poached rabbit with anchovy beignet, and langoustine with braised veal skin and minced veal macaroni.

Phillip Howard

Two-star chef Phillip Howard at The Square in London also raises the bar quite high with such traditional offerings as lasagna of crab with a mousseline of scallops and salmon (2000); loin of venison with pear and peppercorn sauce, roasted foie gras with apple puree, and scallops with cèpes and garlic puree (2004); and a lasagna of Dorset crab with a cappuccino of shellfish and Champagne foam (2009). Howard told us he took some time off to reassess his career goals in 2003 and then rededicated himself to making The Square one of London's finest restaurants.

Brett Graham

The sister restaurant of The Square, the two-star The Ledbury, displays the talents of the brilliant rising star Brett Graham whose cutting-edge cuisine during our 2009 visit included woodcock ravioli with a toast velouté; a ceviche of scallops with seaweed, herb oil, kohlrabi, and frozen horseradish; and a Yorkshire grouse breast and leg with sauces of whiskey and chocolate malt. Since launching the restaurant in 2005 at age twenty-six, Graham has clearly established himself as one of London's chefs to watch.

Fergus Henderson

When they dine out, many London chefs have—for years—made St. John a "do not miss" destination because of its unique selection of organ meats. On our visit there in 2007, we enjoyed such nose-to-tail offal offerings as the pig's head with butter beans, dried salted venison liver, roast bone marrow with parsley salad, tripe with fennel and bacon, and chitterlings with kale mustard greens—totally different from any meal we have ever experienced.

ⵏ◎ⵏ

CHAPTER 10

Other Europe and Asia

We have yet to visit the nine current three-star restaurants in Germany, the four in Belgium and the two in the Netherlands. Similarly, as the Michelin Guides have expanded to Japan and Hong Kong (with Singapore on the radar screen), we can only look forward to experiencing some of those exciting destinations as time permits in the future. Tokyo has become the new hot spot in Asia for creative chefs wishing to push the envelope. Michelin recognized eight three-star Japanese restaurants in its initial publication in 2008, and highlighted an amazing thirty-two three-star restaurants for 2012.

‌⵩◎⵩

CHAPTER 11

Michelin Comes to the United States (New York, San Francisco, and Chicago)

Thomas Keller

For years, Thomas Keller has set the standard for great gourmet cooking in the United States with his flagship restaurant The French Laundry in Napa Valley (seven visits since 1995), and most recently his New York version, Per Se (seven visits). With only thirteen US restaurants ever receiving Michelin three-star recognition, Keller is the owner of two of them concurrently. Using only the highest quality and freshest meat, fish, and vegetables in his thoughtful and attractive presentations, it is said that Keller never duplicates a single ingredient, spice, or seasoning in a meal.

After several visits to the French Laundry, Fat Duck's Heston Blumenthal noted, "It is just possible that the best example of precise, classical French cooking is not in France but in the US." What is amazing is how easily Keller was able to duplicate his great Napa Valley menus in New York without losing a beat in earning three Michelin stars at both locations. The name Per Se was chosen after people asked Keller what he would name the new restaurant in New York. He would reply, "It's not going to be the French Laundry per se."

We have particularly enjoyed Sunday lunches at Per Se, looking out on Central Park from the elegant sunlit room. Keller offers several legendary signature appetizers at both locations, where the menus are often interchangeable. His "Oysters and Pearls" features tapioca with a special imported caviar. He pioneered the famous smoked salmon ice cream cone with crème fraîche, and his scrambled egg with black truffle shavings is served in an eggshell.

The variety of main courses and desserts that follow are accented with artisan breads and served with interesting butters and gourmet salts. The fish, meat, and game are usually attributed to their special farm sources and are always perfectly cooked. "Surf and turf" can take the form of sweetbreads with Scottish langoustines; a lobster pancake will have such creative accompaniments as pea shoots and a sweet, ginger carrot butter; and the highest quality artisan beef may be matched with crispy bone marrow, special wild asparagus, and a rich reduction sauce which is to die for. The desserts are among the best in the world, featuring wonderful fruit sorbets that might be combined with a special rum cake, and a chocolate dessert of some type always appears accompanied by a creative ice cream such as lemongrass. The gourmet chocolate candies served at the end are always a nice touch.

Keller apprenticed in Paris at Guy Savoy and Taillevant before opening Rakel in New York City in 1987. He moved to Napa Valley in 1994 to open the French Laundry, which has become for many the best restaurant in the United States. Both the French Laundry and Per Se, which opened in 2004, were awarded three stars in the first years of the California and New York City Michelin Guides. His cookbook on the French Laundry is considered one of the best cookbooks ever produced in the United States.

Eric Ripert

The other Michelin three-star chefs in New York City are also quite deserving. Chef Eric Ripert at Le Bernardin has established a reputation for serving the most outstanding seafood and fish. Both former *New York Times* food critic Frank Bruni and *New York* magazine have consistently rated Le Bernardin as "the number one restaurant in New York City."

In a somewhat understated and comfortable setting, Ripert makes food the star. The presentations on the plate reflect a true artist at work in the kitchen, with brightly colored sauces and emulsions often featured in spectacular geometric designs. Ripert does not hesitate to accent his fish courses with a little heat from chorizo oil, curry, saffron emulsion, peppercorn pesto, or anchovy sauce, or to put his fish in a consommé or a spiced bamboo broth. Other memorable standards include the peekytoe lump crab cake with a shaved cauliflower and mustard emulsion, a spicy langoustine sambal, a turbot with a shiso maitake soaked in a lemon miso broth, and red snapper baked in a rosemary and thyme salt crust. A recent meal in late 2011 featured seared langoustine with foie gras and a delicious balsamic dressing on mâche and wild mushrooms, and a baked lobster with a whiskey and black peppercorn sauce.

For one interesting lunch at Le Bernardin in 2007 (when I was in town for business by myself), I sat at the counter and talked shop with the "insatiable" food critic Gael Greene. She was still at *New York* magazine at the time and in the restaurant for a photo shoot.

Born in Antibes in France, Ripert cooked at Tour d'Argent and with Robuchon at Jamin early in his career. He moved to the United States in 1989 to apprentice under Jean Louis Palladin in Washington, DC, and David Bouley in New York. Ripert joined Le Bernadin in 1992 and became the executive chef in 1994 at age twenty-nine when the chef suddenly died. He earned a four-star *New York Times* rating in 1995 and three stars from Michelin in 2006. Ripert believes that food connects everyone as a "cultural phenomenon that informs our traditions and our relationship with earth."

Jean Georges Vongerichten

Jean Georges' cooking has always had a special appeal for me. We have enjoyed nine meals over the past fifteen years at his flagship restaurant, Jean-Georges, which has earned three stars since the initial New York City Michelin Guide was published in 2006. His traditional tasting menu features such great individual courses as the egg caviar served in a shell, a classical young garlic soup with thyme and sautéed frog legs, the lobster tartare with lemongrass and fenugreek broth, and broiled squab paired with fois gras and corn pancake. From the changing seasonal menu where his ongoing creativity shines, we remember such interesting courses as his egg toast, caviar and dill; the spicy tuna tartare with black olive and cucumber; and the roasted veal, artichokes, lavender and liquid Parmesan. In 2002, as our son Todd was leaving Clio and Ken Orringer in Boston to move to New York City to join Bouley, Jean Georges' kitchen honored him by preparing one of the best meals I have ever enjoyed in the United States. It included two ten-course tasting menus presented side-by-side with incredibly creative preparations of lobster, foie gras, and lamb.

Born in the Alsace region of France, Vongerichten was influenced by a meal he ate at L'Auberge de l'Ill at age sixteen. He worked there and at Paul Bocuse before moving to the United States in 1985 to cook in Boston and New York. He earned four *New York Times* stars while running the kitchen at Lafayette in 1989 and then opened JoJo in 1991. His greatest recognition came after opening his namesake restaurant in the Trump Tower in 1997, immediately earning four *New York Times* stars with his contemporary interpretations of French cuisine.

Masa Takayama

To earn three Michelin stars, a Japanese sushi bar in the United States has to be something really special, and Masa has become the definitive restaurant for new Japanese cuisine. Located in the Time Warner complex on Columbus Circle adjacent to Per Se, Masa Takayama brings in fresh fish and seafood from all over the world several times a week (often in organ donor bags). Masa and his two sous chefs prepare each course behind an eight-person counter with a seasonal Japanese tree in the background. Even the beautiful Hinoki wood for this $60,000 counter (which is sanded every night after service) was procured from Japan.

Masa's first five courses are substantial and usually include a generous portion of toro (fatty tuna belly meat) tartare with caviar, followed by a selection of either Kobe beef, foie gras, or matsutake mushrooms, often served on risotto or in a shabu

shabu broth. And during certain seasons, blowfish may even be on the menu, served first as the skin, liver, and intestine, and then in a second course tempura-style with the flesh on the bone. On one visit, a noodle course made entirely of homu fish and served with yuzu zest was particularly memorable. Fresh white and black truffles in season are often shaved generously on many of the courses.

Twenty-five to thirty courses of sushi then follow and include several special Japanese maki (rolls) wrapped in a thin, handmade seaweed sheet also imported from Japan. Over our six visits, we have had many memorable and unusual sushi items, including a fresh baby anchovy marinated in saltwater, vinegar and oil; octopus with Himalayan salt; tilefish with white truffles; and even the white cartilage from toro (which is barbecued and softened enough to digest easily. The quality and freshness of the fish justifies, for us, the highest-priced dinner in New York City.

Takayama moved to New York City in 2004 after a highly successful run in Los Angeles. Born in Japan, he got his early training in Tokyo's Ginza district and received three Michelin stars for Masa in 2009.

Daniel Boulud

The highly respected French chef Daniel Boulud finally earned a third Michelin star for his restaurant Daniel in 2010. Since moving to his new location off Park Avenue in 1999, Daniel has offered one of the most elegant dining locations in the United States (although the Greek style columns may be a bit over the top). Nevertheless, this is an improvement over the old location where a shoehorn was often necessary to get into the small two-top tables jammed closely together. Daniel offers outstanding fish dishes, and his desserts are clearly among the best in town. Among our three dinners at Daniel, we especially enjoyed our 2007 meal that included a pea velouté; a crayfish cassoulet with cock's comb tempura, white asparagus and poached egg dressing; and a creative rabbit course that included a braised leg and roasted saddle served with pork belly.

Boulud was born outside Lyon in France and got his early training with Roger Verget, George Blanc, and Michel Guérard. He was the executive chef at Le Cirque in New York City from 1976 to 1992 before opening Daniel in 1993.

Daniel Humm

Daniel Humm of Eleven Madison Park received three well-deserved Michelin stars in the 2012 New York edition (he had already garnered four *New York Times* stars). Humm, who joined Rabeay at Pont de Brent in Switzerland in 1996 and caused quite a positive stir at Campton Place in San Francisco earlier in his career, has quickly become one of New York City's major chefs. His creative tasting menus always contain a number of pleasant surprises such as arctic char roe with baked potato ice cream, a foie gras torchon with Venezuelan cocoa and quince gelée accompanied by a foie gras brûlée, a Chilean turbot served with scales made of baby zucchini or with a shellfish nage and Thai curry, and many perfectly cooked meat courses with interesting accompaniments. This elegant, high-ceilinged restaurant in lower Manhattan provides a unique accent point while experiencing Humm's thoughtful offerings.

Humm started his career cooking at age fourteen in Zurich and moved to San Francisco in 2003. He turned around Eleven Madison Park immediately upon his arrival in 2006 and has now become a part owner. His promotion from one to three Michelin stars in a single year is an unusually dramatic change, but well-deserved. Humm believes in elevating flavors by cooking at low temperatures, especially with the high quality ingredients he uses. He avoids searing fish, which he notes overcooks the outside of the fish.

Chris Kustow

We have loved our two meals with Chris Kustow since he took over the kitchen at the Meadowood Resort in Napa Valley. Getting his third Michelin star in 2010 seemed to be proper recognition of his significant talents.

In 2009, we had our first meal with Kustow. His "Tea and

Crumpets" included mushroom consommé made from a tea bag and accompanied by black truffles and a crumpet with pecorino cheese. His tasting menu included smoked toro with caviar and crème fraîche dots, foie gras four ways (including seared with peanut butter, and in custard), ocean trout cured in a pinecone and served with olive oil cream and crispy artichokes, a poached lobster accompanied by a ravioli stuffed with sweetbreads and foie gras in truffle foam, a sous vide poussin with chorizo and clam, and a rack of baby goat poached in whey with wheatgrass in a broth.

Our second visit in 2011 was just as exciting. Soy-cured foie gras was paired with a pea puree, clams, and periwinkles in cocoa butter; the langoustine was served in a tapioca veil with strips of scallops and pork belly, baby hasimesie mushrooms, and a langoustine broth. The truffle-glazed sweetbreads were accompanied by parsnip puree, black truffles, and a rice chip. The room is understated country elegant, and the staff, with its obvious knowledge and respect for every dish, makes the entire evening seem special.

Kustow is only the second American-born chef to ever earn three stars (Keller is the other) and the third youngest to ever receive this honor. After earning a degree in philosophy from Hamilton College, he cooked at Campton Place and Elizabeth Daniel and later at Jardin de Sens and Chez Georges in France. He moved to Meadowood in 2008 after earning two Michelin stars at Chez TJ in Mountain View (south of San Francisco) in 2006. Kustow tries to create a transcendental experience for diners with his highly innovative combinations of traditional ingredients.

Other Northern California Notables

In northern California, two-star chefs Daniel Patterson of Coi and David Kinch of Manresa are also deserving of three stars. Patterson's brilliance is not fully appreciated by all who dine with him, but we have followed him loyally since his days at Elizabeth Daniel from 2000 to 2004. His courses are often stunning in their presentations, and he can make vegetables seem magical—even a carrot cooked in its own juice. At our most recent dinner, he offered among the fifteen courses: beets roasted in hay and beet puree with cow and goat milk cheeses; a lardo-topped crab melt with a green puree of wheat grass and pea sprouts painting the plate; a slow-cooked egg yolk with egg foam, rosemary, and flowers; and for dessert, a delicious brioche ice cream with chocolate mousse and pistachio crumbles. The Asian atmosphere provides a Zen-like experience so that diners can fully appreciate the cerebral Patterson's subtle creativity, which is self-taught.

In July 2011, Kinch cooked a near-perfect meal for us that included abalone (at our request) two ways (with raw milk pancetta, abalone gelée and abalone slices, and also roasted with a cucumber and avocado moustada); razor clams with a wild rice vinaigrette and chrysanthemum and roast chicken jelly; a "Vegetable Garden" on toasted dark bread crumbs, spot prawns and gooey duck clams in miso broth; a Napa Valley rack of lamb with wild morels and a bitter orange and turnip confit; and a chocolate caramel cream with popcorn custard and fleur de sel ice cream. We still remember an incredible Pennsylvania wood pigeon cooked in a salt crust from a prior visit. The Los Gatos location is a bit out of the way but well worth the trip for a meal with "the surfer chef."

A graduate of the Johnson and Wales culinary academy, Kinch opened Manresa in 2002 after cooking at L'Esperance in France, Akelar̆e in Spain, the Quilted Giraffe in New York City, and traveling extensively in Europe and Japan. His minimalist approach showcases local ingredients, many of which come from Love Apple Farms in nearby Santa Cruz.

One of the most exciting new chefs in San Francisco is French Laundry and Per Se alum Cori Lee, who opened Benu in July 2010 to great success and a two-star Michelin rating for 2012. His obvious talent was displayed in a dazzling tasting menu that included sea urchin with an almond mousse; a sake lees sorbet with foie gras mousse and yuzu foam; eel in a pastry crust resembling a cigarette served on an ashtray; a salt and pepper squid crisp with fermented chili pepper and

Our first visit to Ferran Adrià's elBulli near Roses on Spain's Costa Brava (2000)

In Michel Bras' kitchen in Laguoile, France (2001)

Sue with Provençal chef Edouard Loubet at his former home outside Lourmarin, France (2002)

At Santi Santamaria's Raco de Can Fabes outside Barcelona, Spain (2003)

With Elena Arzak and Todd Macdonald in Restaurant Arzak's "Flavor Bank" of special starches and spices. San Sebastian, Spain (2003)

At Akelaŕe in San Sebastian, Spain with friends Javier Anitua and his wife Sol Ortiz de Artinano (2004)

With Maître d' Christophe Rohat at L'Astrance in Paris (2004)

At Alain Ducasse's Le Louis XV in Monte Carlo (2005)

Our favorite Florence restaurant Cibrèo (2006)

Sue with Rosalind Seysses at Burgundy's Domaine Dujac in Morey St. Denis, France (2006)

With chef
Gerard Rabaey at
Le Pont de Brent in
Brent, Switzerland
(2006)

At Olivier Roellinger's Le Bricourt in Cancale, France (2007)

Sue in the rain at Michel Guérard in Eugénie-Les-Baines, France (2008)

After a Burgundy tasting with Aubert de Villaine at Domaine Romanée Conti in Vosne-Romanée, France (2010)

With Pierre Gagnaire and Butcher and the Boar Minneapolis chef Jack Riebel in Paris (2010)

After frog legs and Bresse chicken at Georges Blanc in Vonnas, France (2011)

dehydrated jalapeño; a monkfish liver torchon with green apple relish; lobster porridge with green curry; black truffle risotto; and a faux shark fin soup with Dungeness crab, black truffle custard and Jinhua ham. In the former Hawthorne Lane location, Lee has transformed the space into an elegant, minimalist environment with earth tones and natural woods—a perfect counterpoint for his brilliant food expressions. Benu means phoenix or rebirth.

One-star chef Michael Tusk has successfully moved his popular Quince restaurant to a larger space. His pastas, including a memorable foie gras tortellini, have become legendary, while nettles and other vegetable-stuffed ravioli and gnocchi often serve as wonderful starters or accompaniments to his thoughtful Italian-style meat courses.

Jöel Robuchon Revisited

After Jöel Robuchon opened his new flagship restaurant in the MGM Grand Hotel in Las Vegas, he immediately earned three stars in this city's first edition of the Michelin Guide in 2008. Such recognition has certainly reinforced his reputation as one of the greatest chefs who has ever lived. While the food is delicious, it is not quite at the same level that Robuchon achieved at his Paris restaurant before it closed in 1996. In April 2009, *Saveur* magazine listed the restaurant as number one of the "12 Restaurants That Matter" (in the United States). His counter oriented L'Atelier, with locations in Paris, London, Hong Kong, New York, and Las Vegas, are also a cut above most gourmet restaurants, and appeal more to the small-plate, bistro-oriented crowd (even earning three Michelin stars in Hong Kong). Robuchon has also opened a Michelin three-star restaurant in Tokyo.

The Robuchon restaurant in Las Vegas has an exemplary kitchen that knows how to cook gourmet food with great finesse, but it is difficult to duplicate the same level of sophistication found in great Paris restaurants, especially since Robuchon is not in the kitchen regularly to ensure perfection. Among our favorite courses enjoyed over Thanksgiving weekend in 2007 were the langoustine ravioli in a sea urchin mousse; a particularly creative oat velouté with chorizo and almonds; turbot with artichoke sauce; and an unusual soybean sprouts course served with chopped soybeans, mushrooms, and chives. Due to financial considerations, Michelin terminated its Las Vegas and Los Angeles guides after 2009.

Grant Achatz

The Michelin Guide finally came to Chicago in 2011 and awarded three stars to the brilliant deconstructionist Grant Achatz, and the mercurial Laurent Gras at L20 (who promptly left for New York a few weeks later). A protégé of Thomas Keller at the French Laundry for four years, Achatz has staked out a claim as possibly the most innovative chef in the United States today. After putting Trio on the map from 2001 to 2004 in the northern suburb of Evanston, he opened Alinea in 2005 to great critical acclaim. His Grand Tour menu can run anywhere from twenty-two to twenty-six courses, and is whimsical in its unusual presentations and deliciously satisfying with multiple combinations of tastes on a single plate. His experimentation with herbs and other unusual ingredients from around the world knows no bounds and might even include the exotic junsai, an Asian water lily harvested from rice pads.

During our eight visits to Alinea, we have enjoyed many wonderful courses, making us eager each time to return for our next meal. His signature dishes include the "Hot Potato/Cold Potato" (cubes of potato cooked with Parmesan, butter, chives, and a slice of black truffle served on a pin that, when pulled out, allows the hot potato cubes to fall into a cold potato soup). The bacon strip flavored with butterscotch and served with a wire through it is also great fun to experience.

A visit in 2008 included short ribs on a Guinness Stout sheet with broccoli and peanut puddings, crispy broccoli tops, cilantro, mustard seeds, and spiced peanuts; foie gras in a plastic tube with black mission fig, tapioca pearls, coffee and tarragon; butter-poached Maine lobster on a dried onion popcorn strip with corn ragout, chanterelle mushrooms, Thai chiles, and a butter capsule; and grade-A5 Japanese Waygu beef with 12-year-old sherry vinegar and Waygu fat vinaigrette, smoked date, and a savory garlic butter.

On our September 2009 visit, we enjoyed several of the signature dishes, plus an opening course of osetra caviar served with deconstructed accompaniments (onion, caper, and lemon distilled jellies, and emulsified egg yolk with grape seed). Among the many creative offerings were foie gras, fennel, and peach on a fork with shiso foam and peach juice in a bowl; and Alaskan king crab in aloe vera gel with a yuzu and sake custard, seaweed, caramelized peanuts, and green tea. The stunner of the night was his tribute to Escoffier: a squab breast and leg quenelle and onion velouté with Périgord truffle sauce in a pastry tart served on an antique plate with an antique wine glass containing a Chateau Palmer Meritage of Cabernet and Syrah, which had been an available wine in 1909.

Achatz's presentations have to be seen and experienced over several meals to appreciate the breadth of creativity and thought that goes into every course. Some of his past courses have included lamb or other meats served on a deflating pillow that was punctured at the table to release aromas of anise, nutmeg, tea, or some fruit essence as it deflates. Once, Achatz served poached lobster in a large bowl, set inside a second larger bowl filled with orange peels that produced floral vapors when hot water was poured on them.

Our most recent meal at Alinea in 2011, offered some new experiences and included a shrimp gumbo with the legs; a gumbo pudding with the head and andouille sausage with the tail; an all-white halibut course served with parsnip puree, vanilla grass, white pepper, coffee, and licorice; a parfait of rabbit mouse with Calvados, apple butter, butternut squash, pumpkin seed, and fried sage; an Escoffier-era duck breast preparation in puff pastry with foie gras, chestnut, black truffle, and Madeira sauce; and his famous dessert medley of frozen chocolate and fruit served directly on a rubber table cloth.

Achatz has also opened a new restaurant called Next, which sells tickets in advance and includes a prepaid tip and wine pairings. His initial menus (which change quarterly) have featured French cooking from the Escoffier era, a Thai tasting menu, and an homage to el Bulli. This is consistent with his philosophy of cooking: create great dishes and then replace them.

Laurent Gras

Awarding L20 three stars was a tribute to Chef Laurent Gras, who unfortunately left before our third meal there in February 2011. There is a lot to like about the elegant, understated, and calming atmosphere and the well-trained service staff. The seasonal tasting menus are thoughtful and creative. In 2011, we enjoyed a combination of salmon and hamachi tartares with yuzu soy, the diver scallop with a passion fruit sauce and caramelized cauliflower, a medley of forest mushrooms with pearl tapioca, perfectly cooked Scottish salmon with a cheese and grits dumpling and Asian spices, and a Wagyu beef filet with tempura-style vegetables. It will be interesting to see what direction the new chef takes this restaurant, which Michelin downgraded to only one star in its 2012 edition.

An earlier visit in 2010 found Gras at his culinary peak, offering his "Spring" and "Singular" tasting menus that included peekytoe crab with foie gras emulsion, yellow fin in shabu shabu broth, toro with osetra caviar and wasabi, and Wagyu beef with black truffle sauce. Our first visit in 2008 still seems the most dazzling because the restaurant was new, and the creative energy was evident in the ten fish courses served as part of the "Summer Tour." The fluke with ginger, jalapeño, and seaberry grapefruit was served in a citrus consommé; the skate was complemented by a Bordelaise sauce, and white and green asparagus; and the Kindai toro had a green apple slice and wasabi emulsion.

Charlie Trotter

Charlie Trotter, who has received two Michelin stars since the initial 2011 Chicago Michelin Guide, has been a change agent for American chefs after opening his own restaurant in 1987. A self-taught chef, Trotter has innovated many of the ways food is presented on a plate (stacking and balancing), and is constantly experimenting with unusual flavor combinations. He was one of the first to feature the artisan sources for his fish and meats on his menu. Trotter's multiple-course tasting menus feature small portions and use a wide variety of sauces and oils prepared in his kitchen. He decided to retire in the summer of 2012.

We enjoyed interacting with Charlie in the early 1990s about our mutual experiences with great French chefs. He seemed particularly intrigued by Gagnaire's seven small plates we had been served before our meal during our 1993 visit to Saint-Étienne. On our next visit to Charlie Trotter, we were informed by the captain that Charlie had something special for us that night. We were then presented with a dazzling display of thirteen small plates for each of the four of us, which filled the table to overflowing—really an unforgettable way of kicking off the wonderful meal that was still to follow. Once all the plates were in front of us, Charlie appeared at the table and simply announced, "Tonight, we are going to f*** the French."

Other Noteworthy Chef Experiences

One of the most ambitious dinners ever held in our Twin Cities community occurred in April 2001 when New York and Minneapolis Aquavit chef Marcus Samuelson hosted the primary dinner for the annual meeting of the International Association of Culinary Professionals. He was able to persuade Chicago-based Charlie Trotter and Tetsuya Wakuda from Melbourne, Australia, to be special guest chefs that evening. The limited list of invitees included several local chefs and foodies, and the meal did not disappoint.

This has been my only chance to sample the legendary Wakuda's food. That evening he prepared his outstanding confit of smoked ocean trout with kombu (kelp) and an incredible carpaccio of scallop with citrus soy jelly. Trotter did a delicious terrine of asparagus and beets with goat cheese and fava bean sauce, and a codfish with braised beef cheek and tongue in a red wine hijiki (black seaweed) sauce. Samuelson offered his Kobe beef ravioli with sea urchin and truffle tea, and a coffee-roasted squab with his signature foie gras ganache and Rhône wine vinaigrette. Aquavit pastry chef Adrianne Odom concluded this memorable evening with a lychee ginger soup served with a rhubarb fennel ravioli, and a poppy seed ice cream sandwich with a chocolate crème brûlée and pine nut foam.

In non-Michelin-reviewed cities in the United States, other chefs are emerging whose reputations will continue to grow. Jose Andres' signature six-seat Mini Bar at Café Atlantico in Washington, DC, and Saam (his private tasting room inside Bazaar restaurant) in Beverly Hills, are deconstructing Spanish cooking in exhilarating ways. Andres' friendship with Ferran Adrià is certainly evident in the exciting courses presented at both venues. Johnny Monis' creative tasting menus at Komi in Washington, DC, have made this an important destination for serious foodies.

The most exciting chefs in the decade of 2011–2020 will include many new well-deserving names not mentioned in this book. This series of reflections is meant as a tribute to those who have made their mark in the prior two decades, and set the stage for other chefs to take new risks and express their artistic talents to a public always looking to be stimulated by new food experiences.

YIOIt

CHAPTER 12

Achieving Three Star Status— What Does It Take?

WHAT MAKES A RESTAURANT WORTHY OF THREE STARS? CER-
tain common characteristics seem to be present in most of
them: an uncompromising attention to the quality of ingredients, and a distinctive style of cooking that can be identified
with the chef. Each generation produces chefs who rise above
their peers to create special signature dishes that define their
reputations and remain memorable and in demand by diners
for years. This does not usually just happen by chance, but
results from a drive and passion to create unique flavors and
courses that diners will talk about long after the meal.

The recent impact of using liquid nitrogen or sous vide (slow
cooking in a pouch to produce a new depth of flavors or textures) are notable advances in cooking techniques. The introduction of peppers and other exotic spices into mainstream
cooking is also just scratching the surface in its potential. There
is reason to believe that the next generation of three-star chefs
will find new techniques and ingredients to achieve dramatic
impact. The food revolution will continue to emphasize freshness of ingredients as heavy sauces and overcooked meats and
fish increasingly become distant legacies of past generations.

PART II

Meeting Grape Expectations

On my tombstone I simply want the words,
"Life is too short to drink bad wine."

More than forty years of wine collecting can create a lot of wonderful memories. I may not have had as great a breadth of experience as a dedicated Frenchman in Burgundy or Bordeaux who grew up with wine as part of their daily lives, or very wealthy collectors who have built or inherited great cellars. Yet, I have endeavored to sample many of the greatest wines made in the twentieth century to try to understand why they are considered so special. The lessons learned and my interaction with other collectors, winemakers, and sommeliers are presented here with great affection.

ꮖ◎ꮖ

CHAPTER 13

Some Thoughts on Choosing and Enjoying Wines

To be able to gain experiences with wine early in one's life provides a valuable benchmark for enjoying other wines from the same country, chateau, domaine, or vineyard that are tasted again years later. This also helps one more fully appreciate how a great wine can really define a meal, and permits the ability to recognize the most intriguing wines and best values on a wine list. Developing this capability is something for which I will always be grateful.

One's enjoyment of wine is often influenced primarily by the circumstances and the place where it is consumed. When describing a special wine experience, people usually vividly remember the occasion, the setting, or the people who helped make the wine so memorable. It is interesting to note that this can often be more important than the characteristics of a wine itself.

I strongly believe that the vintage of a wine is critical, not only in determining how long it will last but how well it is likely to show at any given time in its maturity. Vintages can make a real difference in producing great wines, since even an average winemaker can sometimes make a special wine in a great vintage, whereas a great winemaker may struggle to make a memorable wine in an average or poor vintage. And, ironically, the prices of wines in restaurants and wine stores do not always properly reflect any significant differences in vintages. So, caveat emptor.

Another important differentiator is drinking both white and red wine out of the proper glasses. Riedel and other manufacturers produce specially shaped glasses that enhance the bouquet and flavors of a wine by helping it properly breathe, as well as delivering the liquid to the area of the tongue that can maximize enjoyment. While the tongue can taste sweet, sour, salty, bitter, and savory flavors, our noses can distinguish as many as 10,000 different scents. That is why having a cold or stuffed nose can spoil an evening of wine drinking.

Wine connoisseurs' descriptions of various wines can be a little extreme at times (wet stones, scorched earth, autumn leaves, saddle leather, mushrooms, pencil lead, etc.), although I plead guilty to occasionally using some of these terms myself. A more basic concern should be whether a wine is sound, with the proper balance of fruit and acid. Knowledgeable wine drinkers often use the terms red and black fruit to describe the taste of a red wine based on whether it reminds them more of strawberries and raspberries or blackberries and plums.

I have always been puzzled by many collectors' preferences for young red wines that can be more expensive to purchase currently than older vintages already nearing their peak of maturity. These older wines can often offer much more interesting drinking experiences. While the risk always exists that older wines may have gone "over the hill," the increased amount of enjoyment from the subtle flavors after the tannins have faded usually far outweighs this risk. Many people do not fully appreciate how good a red Bordeaux or Burgundy from a great vintage can taste fifteen to thirty years after bottling. A really great vintage improves the odds that a wine will take longer to reach its peak, and therefore be accessible for enjoyable drinking over a greater period of time.

I seldom order the most expensive wine on a wine list, because it is generally overpriced and more often than not is from an average or mediocre vintage. In France, I try to find hard to obtain Burgundies from the best vintages, which are sometimes available below their retail prices in the United States. Because I believe French white Burgundy is by far the best white wine in the world, I seek out these wines even when traveling in Spain or Italy because they seem more food friendly than the white wines of the local country. I always look for the best value on the list, starting with the greatest vintages for each type of grape, and then look at the producers or domaine from which they come, since the winemaker can sometimes have an even greater influence on quality than the vintage. I set a rough limit for what I will spend on a wine, and this may lead to a family conversation as to whether a possible splurge above this amount is worth it or not.

For white Burgundy, I respect Comte de Lafon, Coche Dury, Michel Niellon, Sauzet, and Ramonet from recent vintages such as 2002, 2004, 2005, 2007, and 2009. And because many recent vintages have displayed problems with their corks causing wines to go bad before their time, I tend to prefer the younger whites. For red Burgundy, many winemakers are currently outstanding, including Domaine Romanée Conti, Domaine Dujac, Comte de Vogue, Meo Camuzet, Georges Roumier, and Freddy Mugnier, as well as larger houses such as Drouhin, Faiveley, Bouchard Père, Louis Jadot and Louis Latour. My favorite red wine Burgundy vintages are 1971, 1978, 1985, 1990, 1996, 1999, 2002, 2005 and 2009. For Chablis, Raveneau and Rene & Vincent Duvaissart made outstanding wines in 1996, 2002, 2005, 2006, and 2009. The first growths of Bordeaux (Lafite, Latour, Mouton, Haut Brion, Margaux) as well as Cheval Blanc and Petrus are especially memorable from the 1945, 1959, 1961, 1982, 1989, 1990, 2000, 2005, and 2009 vintages.

When special wines like Henri Jayer's Vosne-Romanée Cros Parantoux red Burgundy appear on a list, it is an opportunity to make the meal an extraordinary experience. Sometimes this involves a request to the sommelier to ascertain whether he or she is willing to even sell it to us. Generally, when we order two great Burgundies from outstanding producers with a meal in France, the rest of the meal flows like clockwork because the waiters and the kitchen are usually aware of what is happening at our table, and extra effort is made to ensure everything is as enjoyable as possible. This is not necessarily because we are ordering the most expensive wines, but rather because they know they are serving a guest who truly loves and understands wine, has ordered great vintages, and will appreciate them fully.

Such knowledge took a lot of trial and error to accumulate over the years, and it is not something easily passed on to others. People have such different tastes that the personal favorites of each wine lover will be dramatically different by grape variety and geographic area. Ordering wines that will be compatible with food is important, which is why I've chosen to become a Francophile for most of my life. I have found that a great wine complements many types of food, so I am not as concerned with so-called "food and wine pairings," which often are an excuse for restaurants to serve less attractive or less expensive wines with each course.

It is understood that ordering wine in a gourmet restaurant in France (and even in the United States) can be intimidating. A great sommelier, however, can create a positive experience. The sommelier should view his or her role as serving the customer by helping select wines that are ready for drinking and within the diner's budget. A knowledgeable sommelier can quickly gauge the sophistication level of a guest. If asked for a recommendation (which should be regarded as a compliment from a wine connoisseur), the sommelier will often discuss where he or she thinks a wine is in its level of maturity, as well as any potential risks involved in choosing an older vintage from similar bottles he or she has sold or tasted. Taking a risk can also lead to an exciting new experience or discovery, but in any event, a competent sommelier should always leave the diner feeling as if he or she has made a good choice to go with the meal.

᛭◎᛭

CHAPTER 14

Learning about the Great Wines

BEFORE SHARING SOME OF MY RESTAURANT WINE STORIES, I thought it would be interesting to highlight how I learned about wine over the years, including some of my greatest experiences sharing wines with friends. Our earliest wine drinking education began in New York City in the late 1960s, where even the greatest French wines were available for under $20 per bottle. This enabled us to learn about the first-growth Bordeaux and the great Burgundies from Domaine Romanée-Conti, and be able to regularly share even older vintages at dinners and wine-tasting parties with our friends.

Before leaving to live in Singapore at the end of 1970, Sue cooked a whole suckling pig (with an apple in its mouth) for our going away party. The special wine tasting that accompanied the evening included a magnum of 1953 Lafite Rothschild, a 1945 Latour, a 1955 Haut Brion, and a 1959 Le Chambertin Burgundy. With its incredible bouquet and a flavor that I have always described as having hints of raspberries, the 1953 Lafite became my standard for great red wines for many years to follow. The 1945 Latour was like an iron fist with its concentrated flavors, hints of tobacco and leather among the fruit, and a long, lingering aftertaste. We were to enjoy this 1945 Latour again with my mother-in-law and father-in-law at Chez Paul in Chicago a year later; he paid for the dinner but my bill was even bigger when I volunteered to select and pay for the wine.

Our first trip to France together in 1970 included a memorable visit to Domaine Romanée-Conti where I had written a letter to the owner and requested a chance to stop by. To our amazement, he extended an invitation, and we were able to barrel taste the inaugural 1969 vintage of the legendary Le Montrachet white Burgundy and also drink a 1963 Romanée-Conti from the bottle. This red wine was light but delightfully fruity and balanced, despite coming from such a mediocre vintage—a tribute to great winemaking.

In Singapore, in addition to writing my restaurant guide for Singapore Airlines, I published three articles on the appreciation of wine in the local Singapore newspaper, the *Straits Times*. In addition to suggested food pairings were recommendations on what was available in the local retail stores. To poke fun at my British colleagues who were writing articles under Chinese surnames, I tried to select the most stuffy and formal British name I could think of—Roland Girth—for my byline. I purchased wines for the British Tanglin Club's wine cellar and remember enjoying a number of bottles of 1962 Lafite Rothschild, which became our "house wine" for special holidays such as Thanksgiving, Christmas, and Easter celebrated with friends in Singapore.

After moving back to the states in 1973, I continued my membership in the International Wine and Food Society (which I had joined in Singapore) with the Seattle chapter. I was asked to judge several homemade wine contests and had no idea dandelion wine could taste so bad. We found a 1970 Robert Mondavi Reserve Cabernet on sale for $4.50 in the local wine store, and my four cases lasted for several years of memorable drinking. I also acquired some 1967 Chateau Latour that became our holiday and dinner party wine for several years and demonstrated, with its great depth of flavor, how good a Latour from even an average vintage could be.

When we moved to our current home in Minneapolis in 1975, I started a wine-tasting club with Rick Theis, the wine editor of the local newspaper. We did a number of interesting wine tastings, including one comparing the 1973 Lafite Rothschild with the 1973 Sterling California Cabernet Sauvignon. A bottle of each was opened twenty-four hours ahead, two hours ahead, and two minutes ahead of tasting. It was interesting that the wines that enjoyed two hours of breathing were strongly preferred in the blind tastings of both wines.

Membership in our informal tasting group changed regularly and eventually included one of the top wine merchants in the Twin Cities, Jack Farrell. A second group was later formed with other good friends including another highly respected wine retailer, David Anderson. These group gatherings brought together many of the best bottles from our cellars to do vertical tastings of Chateau Margaux, Latour, Lynch Bages, Petrus, George Latour Private Reserve California Cabernet, and an interesting comparison of the first-growth Chateau Haut Brion with its impressive neighbor La Mission Haut Brion across the road. These primarily Bordeaux tastings were a real education for all of us, with the better vintages normally showing the best.

In 1981, I was invited to join the local Twin Cities chapter of the Confrérie des Chevaliers du Tastevin, a society dedicated to French Burgundy and headquartered at the Clos de Vougeot in the heart of the Cote de Nuits north of Beaune. The membership benefited from many special wines that came from Commandeur John Staver's cellar, and which he so generously shared with us. This was also my first exposure to the Dr. Barolet Burgundy wines from the 1930s, including one particularly memorable 1934 Volnay. The port-like characteristics and lingering aftertaste of Barolet's still enjoyable wines are among my greatest Burgundy memories. At another Tastevin dinner, we were able to compare three 1961 wines from the Domaine Romanée Conti: a Richebourg, a LaTache, and a Romanée St. Vivant. An aged DRC wine from a great vintage achieves a depth of fruit flavor that I often describe as elderberry, and a bouquet that one would often be happy to just smell all night—and may never want to finish.

Rare weekends in the 1980s, away from our kids and around our wedding anniversary in January, were usually spent in Napa Valley where we had several wonderful visits to Chateau Montelena. The thoughtful hosts would set up vertical tastings that often included six vintages of their recent Cabernets along with several Chardonnays. On recent visits, the winery has gotten quite commercial, and that wonderful individual attention has long passed into a memory.

In January 1989, we were hosted by the legendary Al Brounstein for a tour of his Diamond Creek vineyards on the mountain road between Napa and Sonoma. This native Minnesotan made some of California's finest wines in the late 1970s and early to mid-1980s. He reportedly brought cuttings of first-growth Bordeaux vines from France on his private plane in 1966 and achieved incredible fruit intensity in his wines by regular cropping and insisting on only natural irrigation.

We walked the grounds of his Volcanic Hill, Red Rock Terrace, Gravelly Meadow, and Lake Vineyards, as he told stories of his early years. Al then asked us to feed bread scraps to the ducks swimming on his small lake. His 1984 Diamond Creek Red Rock Terrace remains the finest California wine I ever tasted in that decade, and I have been fortunate to be able to regularly renew my supply through auction. It is still drinking well today with its concentrated flavors of cassis, violets, and black fruit, and seems much more compatible with food than many of the bigger, less subtle California Cabernets currently being made. I recently purchased nine-liter (twelve-bottle equivalent) and twelve-liter (sixteen-bottle equivalent) bottles of this wine to serve at one of our annual chef's parties at our home.

Most of our wine trips to France in recent years have been to Burgundy, but we did have one very interesting trip to Bordeaux in 1992. After a special tour of Chateau Latour, we went on to an appointment at the wine museum at Mouton Rothschild. Our tour guide was rumored to be the Baron's blonde, sixty-year-old mistress, who wore a red miniskirt that day. Tastings were not always featured during these Bordeaux visits, since our hosts took pride in emphasizing the history of the chateaus and the innovations being taken in growing and cultivating the grapes to improve their quality.

On the day of our twenty-fifth wedding anniversary in January 1993, we had a special visit to the Chalone Vineyard in the Gavilan Mountains west of Monterey, California. The winemaker who hosted us couldn't have been more gracious. We enjoyed barrel tasting all their best red and white wines and appreciated their special gift of an outstanding reserve Chardonnay.

Two watershed events that occurred in the 1990s were an important part of my wine education. The first one occurred on November 12, 1994, at the twentieth anniversary celebration of The Chicago Wine Company held at the Ritz Carlton in Chicago. The pre-dinner tasting was the most impressive collection of French Bordeaux that I will ever have in my life. It included 1945 Mouton Rothschild, 1945 Latour, 1947 Cheval Blanc, 1953 Lafite, 1953 Margaux, 1961 Latour, 1961 Petrus, and 1961 Haut Brion. This was my first experience with the 1945 Mouton Rothschild, which I have come to consider the greatest wine ever made. This is a major concession from a confirmed Burgundy lover. The incredible cascades of Asian spice flavors and an aftertaste bursting with berry fruit, licorice, and leather were hard for my brain to fully process at first. I had never tasted any wine like this in my life. By contrast, the legendary 1947 Cheval Blanc was delicious, but seemed almost one-dimensional compared to the 1945 Mouton.

The 1945 Mouton is such an amazing wine that I later chose to drink it in magnum on the night of my sixtieth birthday celebration at Michel Bras in France (it didn't benefit from riding in my trunk for several days). Another bottle was shared with our winemaker friends Ken and Grace Evenstad, and we were extremely disappointed when it seemed completely maderized. I saved one glass from the bottle to try the next day, and to my amazement, the wine had thrown off its maderization and tasted like the old friend I had enjoyed previously. I have never experienced such a transformation from bad to good happening to that degree with any other wine in more than forty years of wine drinking.

Another major influence was a wine tasting and dinner I was invited to attend with Robert Parker and thirteen of his friends at Le Montrachet in New York City on June 28, 1996. With Master Sommelier Daniel Johnes presiding over the evening, we drank four magnums of Henri Jayer Burgundies from the glorious 1978 vintage. Parker was the center of attention, as expected, with people heavily influenced by his opinions on various wines. Yet it was a very relaxed and outspoken environment because of the obvious wine knowledge of all those attending, including his close friend Bruce Gearhart who had included me in this special evening. The food was understated to emphasize the quality of the wines (the pot-au-feu beef served with the main course is about as neutral as you can get). The 1978 Jayer magnums included Echezeaux, Vosne Romanée from both Les Brules and Cros Parantoux, as well as a Nuit Saint Georges Meurgers. In addition, we had Jayer magnums of 1980 Echezeaux and 1982 Nuit Saint Georges Meurgers. These Jayer wines showed extremely well, and the glorious fruit provided by his low-yielding vineyards made each wine really quite memorable.

When Ken and Grace Evenstad decided to make Pinot Noir wine in Oregon, we were very excited. This offered us a chance to live vicariously through their adventurous undertaking. From their initial vintage in 1990, they have emphasized low yields, and were one of the first wineries in the United States to set up a sorting line for the grapes to ensure that only the best fruit was used in making the wine. They have never compromised this philosophy of quality over quantity. As a result, Domaine Serene has developed an outstanding reputation among its peers in Oregon for making some of the best Pinot Noirs in the United States. This is best evidenced by how many restaurants around the country have told us that they have a hard time keeping the Domaine Serene wines in stock.

The Evenstads built one of the most beautiful wineries in the United States in 2001, a five-level gravity-flow facility that eliminates any need to disturb the wine by pumping. Their 1990 to 2000 vintages were fermented and bottled in a historic 1913 building in nearby Carlton (which had previously been used as a glove factory). I had the opportunity to stand on the narrow wooden plank above the large (6 ft. by 6 ft.) plastic bins and pigeage (push down) with a long plunger to break up the hardening cap that forms on top of the grapes while they are fermenting. I never fell into the vat but the consequences of a false step were not pretty to comprehend.

During the 2005 harvest, Sue and I also had the chance to work their sorting line in the new winery. Trying to spot every unripe grape, or a cluster that a hungry coyote has eaten the bottom off of, can be a very intense experience. The tiny earwigs, which are little green bugs with crab-like pincers, added some discomfort by crawling into our hair and inside our shirts while the grapes were being sorted.

Ken Wright was Domaine Serene's original winemaker until 1997. Tony Rynders, Eleni Papadakis, and Erik Kramer followed in the role. Domaine Serene began offering its first vineyard-designated wine in 1996 named after the Evenstads' son, Mark Bradford. A number of other vineyards have subsequently been added including the spicy, sexy Grace vineyard (my favorite) in 1998, and the specially blended Monogram (Ken's initials) with the 2002 vintage.

Their wines have done quite well in several large blind tastings conducted at the winery, including comparing some younger vintages of 1998 to 2000 to Domaine Romanée-Conti wines from the same vintages. This was quite an impressive achievement, but I have always believed DRC wines need at least ten to fifteen years to really "show their stuff." As a result, I was quite interested to do a blind tasting in 2008 of French Burgundies from the great 1990 red Burgundy vintage with the 1990 Reserve and Evenstad Reserve wines from their initial vintage. Both Domaine Serene wines more than held their own, although the 1990 DRC Richebourg and a 1990 Dujac Bonnes Mares were favored by a small margin in our group of five tasters in the summer of 2008.

In 2009, six of us, including Domaine Serene's winemaker, Eleni Papadakis, blind tasted four French Burgundies from the exemplary 1996 vintage, including La Tache, against Domaine Serene's 1996 Evenstad Reserve and the initial release that year of its Mark Bradford vineyard. All the wines were delicious, but in a result that was stunning to me, the Mark Bradford was unanimously chosen as the top wine with its attractive bouquet, pure cassis flavors, and lingering fruit aftertaste. The La Tache, which may have suffered from a marginal cork, still showed great structure and came in second. The Domaine Serene Evenstad Reserve, Comte de Vogue Bonnes Mares, the Dujac Bonnes Mares, and the Anne Gros Richebourg all were delicious but showed less favorably than the first two wines.

The greatest Burgundy wine I have ever tasted was a 1959 La Tache from DRC at the Evenstad's home in December 1996, where it was also shared with winemaker Ken Wright and our friends Chris and Marian Levy. It was the most memorable Burgundy I have ever tasted with a beautiful bright color, deep aromatic bouquet, a perfect balance of fruit and acid, and a complex lingering aftertaste. I have talked to other Burgundy lovers who agree that the 1959 La Tache has had a similar impact on them as well.

In the spring of 1999, our friend Steve O'Hara, who is in one of my wine groups, hosted a vertical tasting of twenty-two vintages of Penfolds Grange Hermitage at our local country club. Made from the Shiraz grape (which had its origins with the Syrah grape in the Northern Rhône region of southeast France), the Grange Hermitage has long set the standard for Australian wines. This two-day event included most of the vintages between 1963 and 1992. This undertaking was really quite overwhelming in its scope, and people's favorites varied widely. The highest-rated Parker vintages (1976, 1986, and 1992) showed well, but my personal favorite by far was the 1989; everyone agreed it tasted much different from the other twenty-one vintages. It had a unique, sweet, and complex flavor of cherries and blackberries, and an incredibly satisfying spicy aftertaste that made this a very special discovery for me. I have continued to successfully seek out this vintage at auctions on several occasions.

A tasting of French Bordeaux wines from the great 1982 vintage is always a special occasion. In October 1999, one of our wine groups tasted most of the first growths, plus Cheval Blanc and Lynch Bages, with an excellent meal from chef Ferris Shiffer at our country club, Minikahda. We voted Cheval Blanc, Lafite, Latour, and Mouton as best, in that order. We revisited the 1982s in December 2004 at another great local restaurant, Restaurant Alma with chef Alex Roberts, and again Cheval Blanc came in first with Latour moving into the second spot. Even the presence of Petrus and Chateau Margaux in the second tasting did not affect the result.

The Cheval Blanc was the clear winner in both tastings with its accessible style, excellent balance, and lingering aftertaste. It was a bit surprising that a wine that is 57% Cabernet Franc and 40% Merlot could command this respect, but the vineyard was on a real roll in 1982. The Latour was beginning to open up, while the legendary 1982 Mouton (likely made for the long term) still seemed many years away from its peak.

We planned a special millennium dinner to usher in the new century on December 31, 1999, for the Evenstads, O'Haras, and Levys. The all-French lineup of wines included a 1986 Raveneau Montee de Tonnerre Chablis, a 1992 Comte de Lafon Meursault Genevrieres, a 1961 Haut Brion, a 1970 Chateau Latour, a 1969 LaTache, a 1971 Richebourg, and a 1959 Chateau d'Yquem that made the evening especially memorable. This 1959 vintage d'Yquem remains the greatest sweet wine I have ever tasted. The complexity that age brings to d'Yquem in such an outstanding vintage is amazing, with cascading layers of fruit and floral flavors.

Sue hosted another special dinner in October of 2000 for several friends who included the Howard Stackers, Evenstads, and O'Haras. After a 1985 Krug Champagne and a 1990 Pol Roget Churchill Champagne, we had the special 1995 Comte de Lafon Le Montrachet, the legendary Spanish 1968 Vega Sicilia (my all-time-favorite Spanish wine), a 1947 LaTache, and a 1970 Chateau d'Yquem. Unfortunately, the La Tache was past its peak, so we did not get to fully experience how great this highly respected trophy wine must have been at one time.

Shortly after returning from France where we celebrated my sixtieth birthday at Michel Bras in October 2001, we had another special celebration with local Minneapolis James Beard-award-winning chef Alex Roberts of Restaurant Alma, who has the same birthday and was also turning a new decade.

With his twin brother, their girlfriends, and his mother joining us, we enjoyed a great dinner at his restaurant, cooked by his capable staff. The selection of special wines included three from his birth year: 1971 DRC Romanée Conti, 1971 Clos Vougeot from Jadot, and 1971 Chateau d'Yquem. That evening we also consumed a 1985 Krug and 1990 Grand Dame Champagne, 1996 Comte de Lafon Meursault Charmes, and a 1996 Le Montrachet Laguiche from Drouhin. The Romanée-Conti was quite spectacular and showed well after thirty years, with subtle fruit intensity, adequate acid, and a perfect balance. Alex still talks about this as his greatest wine memory. In October 2011 on my seventieth birthday and Alex's fortieth, we shared a delicious 1991 Romanée-Conti and another bottle of 1971 Chateau d'Yquem. Both wines showed their full potentials.

Another wonderful experience we shared with the Evenstads was the "1928 Tasting" at our home in December 2002. After researching all the pre-World War II Bordeaux vintages, I concluded that 1928 was perhaps the greatest year and Chateau Latour, which is usually made of 100% Cabernet Sauvignon grapes, would be the longest lived of all of the Bordeaux wines. (Bordeaux wines usually outlast red Burgundy wines from the same vintages.) It took me more than a year to secure the 1928 Latour and then, by chance, I was also able to obtain a 1928 La Tour Blanche Sauterne that made for a very interesting evening celebrating this legendary vintage.

After a delicious foie gras torchon with the subtle, satisfying, and still sweet 1928 La Tour Blanche, we enjoyed a rack of lamb with the 1928 Latour, which had been recorked under vacuum at the winery. We found this seventy-one-year-old red wine to be quite fresh with a wonderful, subtle bouquet, soft tannins, and a glorious understated fruit intensity that lingered for many seconds on the palate in the aftertaste. We all felt this bottle might have still have another fifty years of life in the future before beginning to meaningfully decline.

Some of my best Italian wine experiences (other than drinking a perfect 1990 Lisini Brunello at Cibrèo in Florence) have been the result of the generosity of my friend Howard Stacker at wine tastings he has hosted. My first experience with the Super Tuscans was a 1985 tasting that highlighted the greatest Sassicaia I will probably ever drink, as well as a memorable Solaia and a Fontalloro with the 100% Sangiovese grape.

Howard insisted on following this up with a 1990 Super Tuscan evening for comparison, and the Solaia was the star, with the Sassacaia, Ornellaia, and Flaccianello della Pierre showing quite well. Subsequently, we were treated to an all-Brunello tasting of 1990s. It was a great surprise to us all that the Lisini was everyone's favorite over both the highly respected Soldera Case Basse and Poggio Antico in this amazing collection of thirteen classic Sangiovese wines.

Our two sons have been raised on great wines since their "inauguration luncheon" at Lutèce in New York City in 1983 when they were eleven and nine years old. The restaurant didn't even ask if it should pour them the French white Burgundy we had ordered. Both of them continued to be exposed to some special wines as they were growing up. While they were still teenagers, I received a shipment one day that included a 1969 DRC Richebourg where the cork under the capsule had almost completely disintegrated into black mush. We decided not to store it but to open it immediately without giving it any rest. Apparently the bottom of the cork retained enough of a seal to preserve the great elderberry bouquet and luscious mouth feel that makes DRC wine unique from any other red Burgundy. It was one of these defining moments when a great wine shows itself so well when least expected, especially since most old red wines usually require the benefit of several months of rest after shipment. Our sons still talk about this as their first great red wine experience.

The 1974 Heitz Martha's Vineyard from Todd's birth year may be the greatest California wine ever made. Its food-friendly understated style, with a hint of eucalyptus from the trees surrounding the vineyard have made this especially memorable on the several occasions we have been fortunate enough to share a bottle. This included a special bottle I had been saving for Todd to honor a landmark event in his life.

In 1997, we revisited Domaine Romanée-Conti (with our sons this time) and were invited to barrel taste all of the 1995s (except for LaTache and Romanée Conti). Winemaker Bernard Noblet spoke mostly French but it was a valuable learning experience for all of us. We were also invited to taste from bottles the 1994 Romanée St. Vivant and the 1992 Grands-Echezeaux, as well as a very special 1975 Romanée-Conti that had mushroom nuances and surprising fruit with hints of rose petals. Aubert de Villaine later told us they had not released any of this wine of late, but kept it to share with special guests. To celebrate the visit, for Christmas in 1998 I gave each son a bottle of the 1995 DRC Richebourg that they had tasted in the barrel.

We began visiting Burgundy on a more regular basis beginning in 2002. Part of the fun has been getting to know Jacques and Rosalind Seysses at Domaine Dujac. Sue and I and our sons have been privileged to have lunch in their home at the domaine several times. Ros is an American who visited Burgundy for the harvest in the early 1970s and married Jacques several years later. These visits have provided some of our most enjoyable wine experiences. I will never forget the first meal of a Bresse chicken served with a 1985 Dujac Clos de la Roche. Subsequent meals have always been delicious with wonderful hearty food—and the challenge to sometimes guess the surprise wine coming up from their cellar to be opened for the meal.

With a pot-au-feu, we were served the Dujac Grand Cru Clos St. Denis wines from the 1976 and 1990 vintages, as well as a 1993 Clos de la Roche. On one occasion, Aubert de Villaine stopped by for lunch and it was interesting to hear his opinions on some of his favorite vintages produced at his Romanée-Conti domaine. He and Jacques are especially fond of their 1991 vintage wines because it was such a challenging year in which to make good wine in Burgundy. Both of them were quite reflective on where the wine market was heading with its insanely high prices for the great 2005 Burgundy reds. We all wondered who would be buying these recent vintages, but I focused for a few years at least on Dujac's 1996 vintage, which I truly love. Jacques' oldest son Jeremy has increasingly taken over the role of lead wine-maker to carry on the family tradition. And like his father, Jeremy has married an American woman, Diana Snowden, whose parents own a Cabernet Sauvignon winery in California.

On our next visit to Romanée-Conti in 2003, we were able to barrel taste all the great 2002s including LaTache and Romanée-Conti, which were showing extremely well in the barrel at that time. At a tasting after the tour we enjoyed a 1996 Le Montra-chet, which was the highlight for Sue as one of the greatest white wines of her life. We also tasted a 1977 Echezeaux and a 1990 Romanée St. Vivant from the bottle.

On our 2006 visit to DRC, we observed the winemaker Ber-nard Noblet emerging head first out of the deep wine vat, appar-ently without any clothes on. The bikini underwear finally appeared, but this was a little too dramatic for Sue. So the great domaines still do stomp the grapes manually. We discussed the 1991 DRC vintage with one of Aubert's assistants who conducted the tour. He then shared a bottle of the 1991 LaTache with us, along with a special 2003 DRC Batard Montrachet white Bur-gundy that is not normally sold outside the winery.

In 2010, Aubert was available to host us personally for a tast-ing of wines opened earlier in the day for a government leader from Hong Kong. We were asked to guess the first wine, which tasted quite young. I guessed 2006 Romanée St. Vivant and was lucky to get it right. A memorable 1990 Grand Echezeaux and a 1997 Batard Montrachet followed, the latter of which is still available only at the domaine. Aubert is one of the real gentle-men in the wine profession and highly respected by everyone who knows him. He has an American wife and is a frequent visitor to major wine and food events in the United States.

Alex Gambal is the only American making wine in Bur-gundy. After moving to Beaune with his family in 1993 to help another American, Becky Wasserman, broker Burgundy wines from small producers to merchants in the United States and elsewhere, Gambal began producing his own wines in 1996 from semi-finished wine, and subsequently from grapes he pur-chased. Moving from a modest winery on the edge of Beaune where he made as many as fifty different red and white Burgundies in 1999, Gambal eventually purchased the Bouchard Ainé property on the Periphérique so as to be able to increase production to his current range of 45,000 to 60,000 bottles per year.

We met Gambal originally at the Oregon Pinot Noir festival, and have subsequently had several pleasant evenings with him and his new wife Diana at Ma Cuisine in Beaune, and at their thirteenth-century farmhouse in the countryside outside the city. The spectacular, two-storied living room was originally a barn for the animals. We enjoyed some very special wines on an October 2008 visit, including a 1990 Corton Charlemagne from Domaine Bonneau du Martray with the curried carrot soup and the classic 1991 Armand Rousseau Le Chambertin and a 1992 Freddy Mugnier Musigny with the veal chops.

I have become a big fan of Gambal's wines because he closely manages the quality of the grapes he is purchasing from the various vineyards and makes his reds in the traditional unfiltered, unfined style. Among our favorite reds are his Vosne Romanée Les Monts from just above La Tache, Echezeaux (2005 was his final vintage from one source), Clos Vougeot (taken from the premium upper-level parcels near the Clos), his Chambertin-Clos de Beze (I would drink the 1999 on my knees), and the perfumy Chambolle Musigny made from old vines. The whites that have received the greatest attention include his Corton Charlemagne, Chassagne Montrachet, Puligny Montrachet, Meursault Maltroie, and "a killer" Bourgogne Blanc Special Cuvee (which is a real bargain because some special grapes are added). He recently purchased land in Batard Montrachet and produced his first vintage in 2011.

Every visit to a world-class winemaker in Burgundy can become a unique memory for someone who loves Burgundy as much as I do. Our invitation to Michel Niellon's cellars in Chassagne-Montrachet was no exception. Since Michel does not speak any English, we hired a local translator to accompany us. We tasted a number of wonderful 2002 vintage white wines as we stood among the wine barrels in his cave. Our translator was having as much fun as we were, and on one occasion he and Michel went on for almost five minutes in French without a word of English ever being translated for us. It must have been a very interesting topic, but we will never know. Michel is an exceptionally gracious man with a twinkle in his eye and a good heart. We consider him one of the special people in Burgundy, and his Batard-Montrachet and Chevalier Montrachet are considered otherworldly wines.

A visit to Laurent Ponsot's Winery in the hills above Morey St. Denis can be a bizarre experience. Ponsot is a self-proclaimed maverick with hair down to his shoulders who rides motorcycles across the United States on his vacations and takes delight in offering blunt, irreverent, and outspoken opinions.

He agreed to receive us in October 2005 and upon our arrival promptly insulted my gift of a Domaine Serene Oregon Pinot Noir as not being "the real" Pinot Noir that could be found only in Burgundy. Our brief tour included a viewing of his antique, hand-cranked wine press from pre-World War II days that is still in use, and a statement that he usually "did nothing with the grapes in his fermentation tanks until after Easter each year." His primary underground storage room has one wall completely exposed to the soil of the vineyard, where the deep roots of the vines planted above are visible.

Ponsot became more cordial once we sat in his visitor room upstairs, and he realized the depth of our knowledge and genuine interest in Burgundies. He acknowledges being "the lone wolf" of the Burgundy winemakers, but it was soon apparent how much he cares about his wines. A half-hour visit soon turned into an hour and a half, and he got so excited at one point that he went to his cellar and brought back one of his special 2002 Clos de la Roche wines from his signature vineyard (1985 Clos de la Roche is the legendary wine of his lifetime). I have since procured two bottles of this 2002 wine for future enjoyment. During the huge run-up in prices for the subsequent 2005 red Burgundy vintage, his Ponsot Clos de la Roche was selling for as much as $1,400 per bottle. This was a fun morning, and Sue and I still laugh about our highly entertaining give-and-take with this unique individual.

The Evenstads invited us to a wonderful wine event in Naples, Florida, in April 2004 where a vertical tasting of LaTache from the 1985, 1988, 1989, 1990, 1992, 1993, 1994, 1995, and 1996 vintages was presented by one of the owners of DRC's exclusive US importer, Wilson Daniels. Not surprisingly, the 1990, 1995, and 1996 showed especially well as outstanding vintages. The dinner that followed at the Blue Provence Restaurant included a spectacular lineup of Bordeaux wines including 1975 Pichon Lalande, 1975 Léoville-Las-Cases, 1961 Lafite Rothschild, and 1953 Pichon Lalande, as well as the rare 1992 white wine from Haut Brion.

One of the most successful wine festivals and auctions in the United States is held in Naples, Florida, every winter and features wines, winemakers, and chefs from around the world. The first night is dedicated to a large-scale wine tasting of over one hundred wines, including a nice selection of French, Italian, and Spanish offerings and a unique opportunity to taste such cult California wines as Harlan, Grace Family, Staglin, and Colgin. To be able to compare these super-expensive wines to each other is not something the average consumer gets a chance to do very often.

We attended this festival in January 2006 as guests of Grace Evenstad (who was chairing the entire event). The second night featured a dinner in their home with New Orleans chef Emeril Lagasse and his staff in the kitchen to prepare a traditional Cajun meal. Emeril surprised us with a special risotto and black truffle course matched with a Mark Bradford vineyard wine from Domaine Serene. The evening was also the much-heralded release of the first vintage (2002) of the special Monogram Pinot Noir, selected each year from the best grapes on the Domaine Serene property. Decanted five times, the wine obviously showed some major tannins but offered a complexity of flavors, a wonderful bouquet, and a lingering aftertaste that provided a great accent point to the evening.

A very talented New Orleans jazz band was reassembled for the first time since Hurricane Katrina and received huge ovations when it played "When the Saints Go Marching In" and other great local jazz standards. (Emeril played drums using his pots and pans). I especially loved the music coming from the well-used, dented tuba that had several radio station stickers pasted inside.

Our fortieth wedding anniversary in January 2008 was spent with our sons and their girlfriends on the Island of Nevis in the West Indies in the Caribbean. It was a great week of walking the beach, deep-sea fishing, and hiking through a rain forest up a 3,300-foot volcanic mountain in the middle of the island. To drink with our anniversary dinner (that Todd the chef cooked), the boys surprised us with two bottles of 1968 Rioja (a red and a white from R. Lopez de Heredia—the Viña Tondonia) from our anniversary year. These were a nice match for the kingfish, red snapper, jerk chicken, red beans and rice, and fried plantains. The white still displayed some hints of fruit after forty years, and the red had soft tannins and enough acid to provide a lingering aftertaste that made it memorable.

An initial trip to the Piedmont area of Italy in September 2010 was long overdue and turned out to be very special. I was fortunate enough to have as a client Leonardo LoCascio of the East Coast importer Winebow. When Leonardo offered to set us up with several special VIP tastings, we jumped at the chance. In addition to the renowned Bruno Giacosa winery, we also asked to visit Roberto Voerzio in La Morra. I had heard much about his colorful personality and the outstanding wines he produces with low yields (sometimes one cluster per vine).

Voerzio's Barolos have achieved cult status because of the concentration and incredible fruit extraction he gets from his grapes. We were initially told that Roberto did not speak any English, so his son would have to host our visit. When I volunteered to bring along a translator in order to meet Roberto, the plans were set. We could not find his house at first, despite directions from several townspeople, but we finally saw him standing outside on his driveway. When we asked if the translator had arrived yet, he didn't know anything about such an arrangement. It turned out (as can be typical in Italy), that the translator had the wrong month on his calendar.

Roberto, in fact, spoke quite good English but probably does not want visitors from outside Italy to know this. He was accessible and friendly in his greeting, but I sensed he might be wondering how much we really knew about wine. I quickly put his mind at ease by mentioning the 1989 Voerzio La Serra in my cellar—one of his very favorite Piedmont vintages. We did a brief tour of the winery before adjourning to the tasting room where he had a wonderful selection of wines waiting for us to taste. These included his 2006 Barolo Brunate, 2005 Barolo Cerequio, 2005 Barbera Riserva Pozzo Anunnuziata, and a not yet released 2003 Barolo Fossati Case (the black cows) that was truly unique in its fruit flavors.

Accompanying these wonderful wines was a bright yellow wheel of Parmigiano-Reggiano that had probably been bartered from a boutique cheese maker. Even Roberto's dog eagerly waited for a few slices of this incredible cheese. At the end of the hour, Roberto's wife stopped by to say hello. (Unfortunately, she has since passed away). As we left, Roberto insisted that I e-mail him my impressions of the 1989 La Serra. I later told him we drank it on Christmas Eve, and that Voerzio Barolos would become part of our Christmas Eve tradition for many years to come. He is a wonderful man and charming host.

⫦◎⫧

CHAPTER 15

Wine Lists, Sommeliers, and Special Memories

WHILE I AM WELL AWARE THAT DESCRIBING THESE VARIOUS wine experiences on which I cut my teeth may be interesting mostly to serious collectors who are familiar with these various wines and vintages, I wanted to put into context how my knowledge has accumulated to allow me to read a wine list with some degree of understanding. This also provides an important perspective for our reactions to several good and bad wine experiences we have had with sommeliers in restaurants around the world.

Most of our encounters have been highly positive, but we do run into the occasional sommelier who is not only condescending, but aggressively managing the cellar and protecting the special trophy wines. This is important because a bad experience when ordering wine can quickly diminish the entire enjoyment of a meal. Some French sommeliers still expect the American consumer in front of them to have little knowledge, so the selection and ordering process can become a "blood sport."

The first time I really became aware of how blatant this could be was at the beautiful resort Villa d'Este on Lake Como in Italy in September 1995. The sommelier moved me off a great Chianti vintage I had ordered to a more recent average vintage that he claimed was "more ready to drink." The wine was mediocre, and this made me a lot more cautious about blindly trusting in the judgment of sommeliers, many of whom did not have my same depth of knowledge or experience with great wines.

Our only really unpleasant experience before that had been in September 1993 at Chevre d'Or in Èze Village on the French Riviera (which now has a two-star rating). After we ordered a Grand Cru Mazi Chambertin from Faiveley, the wine arrived at the table already opened, and the sommelier began pouring without ever showing me the label. When I asked to see the bottle, it was not the vintage I had ordered from the wine list but a very mediocre 1981. The sommelier was obviously embarrassed and immediately removed the bottle and our glasses from the table, eventually bringing another a wine that was not the one we had ordered either.

A number of our most memorable "battles" have been in the restaurants of Alain Ducasse in Monte Carlo, New York, and Paris. Our first encounter came in April 2000 at the wonderful Louis XV in Monte Carlo while attempting to order a 1996 Comte de Lafon Meursault Charmes, one of our favorite white Burgundies that always displays beautiful fruit and vanillin flavors. The sommelier kept directing me to other white wines, but having the chance to drink one of the Lafon Meursaults with our great meals in France had become a real priority for us. I finally had to tell him about all the Lafon wines I had collected in my own cellar including 1995, 1996, and 1997 Le Montrachets—the Holy Grail for many collectors. Only at this point did he relent and let us have our bottle of Meursault Charmes, and he was really quite pleasant throughout the rest of the meal.

I began to realize how consistent the training of Ducasse's sommeliers must be when I tried to order the same Lafon Meursault Charmes several years later at Ducasse's elegant new restaurant on Central Park South in New York City. My efforts were aggressively rebuffed, and the sommelier would not relent until he had steered me to a Lafon Meursault village wine that was allegedly "more ready to drink." I asked him why a restaurant would choose to put a wine on its list if it was not yet ready to drink and they had no intention of selling it. I did not get a straight answer, but it seems I was not enough of a regular customer to merit ordering this special wine that he could not easily replace once it was gone.

If this encounter with a Ducasse sommelier in New York City was not enough evidence, our second visit there was one of the worst disasters I have ever experienced in a restaurant. It became so outrageous that I felt a need to write a personal letter to Ducasse outlining what had happened. Ducasse replied very promptly with a thoughtful, handwritten note offering a free bottle of Champagne on our next visit, which we had no intention of ever collecting. Three of the four bottles of wine we ordered that evening came with unpleasant confrontations or misrepresentations.

The 1996 Sauzet Village Puligny Montrachet was badly corked (as many white wines unfortunately were in this Burgundy vintage), and only after we had to ask the sommelier to taste the wine did he actually acknowledge that he was having real problems with all the bottles from that case of wine. For a replacement white village Burgundy wine, we were not told the price and were charged considerably more. Another wine we had ordered was suddenly not available as the food arrived, and the same wine from a much less attractive vintage was brought to the table. When the bill arrived, we were charged $20 over the price on the wine list for a third bottle (which was acknowledged and corrected when I asked the waiter to check).

So when we later visited Ducasse's three-star restaurant in Paris for the second time (and our first time at his new location at the Hôtel Plaza Athénée) in March 2006, I didn't know what to expect. The sommelier immediately took control and did everything in his power to steer me from the legendary 1988 Henri Jayer Vosne Romanée Cros Parantoux to a 1988 Meo Camuzet Vosne Romanée Chaumes. By this time, nothing that Ducasse's sommeliers did surprised me.

Ironically, this 1988 Henri Jayer Vosne Romanée Cros Parantoux wine has provided many of our greatest red Burgundy memories in restaurants around the world. As many Burgundy lovers know, this wine has become one of the true classics produced in the last thirty years. We have been fortunate enough to have had this wine thirteen times in restaurants since 1995, and it has provided some incredible memories when paired with great food. It is a wine of classic elegance with a glorious, structured bouquet, and a perfect balance of fruit and acid. I have always believed it is a privilege to drink this Jayer wine, made by a winemaker so highly respected by his peers. Most important to Burgundy historians, 1988 is reputed to have been the last vintage in which Henri Jayer actually drove his tractor into the field to both harvest the grapes and prune the vines prior to harvest.

Our first bottle was enjoyed in May 1995 at the two-star Auberge de Templiers in Les Brezards near the Loire Valley in Central France. At the time, the Jayer wines on the wine lists in France were still priced well below the Domaine Romanée-Conti wines, which had been my standard until then for excellence in French Burgundies. Jayer's wines are lighter in color and more elegant in style than the DRCs, which usually mature into bolder, deeper, and sometimes more complex fruit flavors. Our first Jayer wine was a revelation that this was really serious Burgundy by a winemaker who understood how to grow the best grapes and get the most out of the wines he made.

In 1997, we next enjoyed the 1988 Cros Parantoux at the three-star Cote St. Jacques in April, and again on my birthday in October of that year at the three-star Jardin des Sens in Montpellier. The quality was consistently great, and I was thankful to find it appearing regularly at an affordable price on so many wine lists of the great French restaurants.

The wine was also on the list at the trend-setting Charlie Trotter's restaurant in Chicago. We had become acquainted with the knowledgeable sommelier Robert Houde on several prior visits, and in November 1999, Houde provided the most generous gesture we have ever experienced from a sommelier. When he felt the first two bottles were corked or flawed in some way, he opened a third bottle for us without hesitating. At almost $800 per bottle at the time (the price had begun to escalate), this was a breathtaking display of thoughtfulness. We have had the 1988 Jayer Cros Parantoux three times at Michel Bras (in 1999, on my sixtieth birthday in 2001, and again in 2003). The three-star Lameloise, just south of the Burgundy vineyards in Chagny, provided the opportunity in October 2000 to enjoy the 1988 Cros Parantoux, and a visit to the two-star Apicius in Paris in April 2003 offered this increasingly hard-to-find gem at a real bargain price of under $400.

During 2004 we had three more opportunities to enjoy the wine. On our first visit to Restaurant Cru in New York City, which received one Michelin star and three *New York Times* stars, and where our son Todd had helped open the restaurant as Shea Gallante's sous chef, the $1,400 per bottle price was still below the escalating retail value at the time. This was a special evening for everyone, and tastes of the wine were shared with various people involved in the restaurant. Before closing in August 2010, Cru prided itself on offering one of the largest wine selections of any restaurant in the United States.

Our France trip in the fall of 2004 enabled us to have the 1988 Cros Parantoux back-to-back on two consecutive days! Unbelievable! We enjoyed it for lunch at the three-star Taillevent restaurant in Paris and then again the next night at the three-star L'Esperance in Vezelay (unfortunately, both restaurants now have only two stars). The wine continued to show uniformly well during all these tastings.

On our October 2005 France trip with our sons, we ordered the wine at the three-star Troisgros restaurant in Roanne. Chef Michel Troisgros was so energized when he heard we had ordered Jayer's 1988 Cros Parantoux that he cooked a special wild hare with cherries and leeks course (to add to our already substantial tasting menu) to enjoy with the wine. It seems particularly fitting to have had such a special course by which to remember this treasure of a wine, since we have not had it again since.

We noted earlier that the sommelier at Alain Ducasse in Paris in 2006 made every effort to dissuade us away from the 1988 Jayer Cros Parantoux. The next night at Taillevent celebrating Sue's sixtieth birthday, it seemed more than a coincidence that a different sommelier (from the one with whom we had worked in 2004) was just as adamant that the 1988 Cros Parantoux "was not doing well" and moved us to a 1990 Meo Camuzet Richebourg.

Do I have any regrets about not pushing harder to get this

wine one more time in 2006? Not really, because we have had so many wonderful bottles, and the retail price had increased to over $2,000 per bottle. As the Cros Parantoux becomes increasingly rare, it is likely that we will never drink it again. But for two independent sommeliers to protect their wine list so aggressively registered clearly with me that on the legendary Burgundies, the wine consumer can expect anything to happen.

As a result of these experiences in 2006 in Paris, I was better prepared for a situation that arose at the recently recognized three-star restaurant at the Hotel Meurice in Paris in April of 2007. When I ordered a rare and special 2002 Vincent Dauvissat Les Clos Grand Cru Chablis, the sommelier informed me the wine was too young to drink. With our recent interchanges still fresh in my memory and having now had my fill of overly controlling sommeliers, I simply looked at him and said, "I would like it, please." He never talked to us the rest of the evening.

We have had so many positive wine experiences in France. Our first great meal in France at La Côte D'Or in 1970 (pre-Bernard Loiseau) was made even more memorable by the 1961 Bouchard Pere Le Montrachet that became our benchmark white wine for many years. For Champagne, a 1961 Florens-Louis Blanc de Blanc from Piper-Heidsieck enjoyed on that same trip at Auberge de Pere Bise on Lake Talloires in the French Alps still remains one of the great Champagne memories of my life.

It is wonderful when a sommelier opens up his cellar for you to try something unique. On our first visit to two-star Brittany chef Jacques Thorel's Le Bretagne in Roche Bernard in May 1998, things got interesting after we ordered the legendary 1985 Krug Champagne. The sommelier asked if we would like to try a 1943 Meursault Charmes from Raoul Clerget. Although the wine was slightly maderized with a orangeish tint, its fruit flavors still came through in a pleasant way, and it proved to be quite memorable and an excellent complement to the lobster and cheese courses.

We have enjoyed many great wines at Jacques and Solange's restaurant over the years. He regards the wines in his great wine cellar as "his children." On subsequent trips, we have had the definitive 1989 Comte de Lafon Meursault Perrières several times, and a 1980 Domaine Dujac Clos de la Roche, drinking at its peak. Since Jacques is quite found of California Chardonnays, on each trip we try to bring him interesting bottles to which he has no ready access. He has now had a chance to try Chardonnays made by Marcassin, Pahlmeyer, Kistler, Peter Michael, as well as the unique Coeur Blanc white wine made from Pinot Noir grapes by Domaine Serene in Oregon. We have also been on the receiving end of some generous gifts of French wine from Jacques, including an unforgettably complex 1970 Vouvray Le Haut Lieu from Domaine Huet that was amazingly fresh and fruity after thirty-five years. It was particularly fun to share this with appreciative friends back home who had never experienced a Loire wine with this much age.

Out of our friendship with Jacques and Solange came an invitation to their cottage on the Breton Coast for a very special lunch in May 2003. This included some deep ocean Breton oysters served from shells almost a foot wide that had to be opened with a sledgehammer, fifty poached baby langoustines, and wonderful assorted cheeses. The memorable complement of wines included a 1989 Chavignol Sancerre from Gerard Boulay and an unforgettable 1964 Armand Rousseau Chambertin Clos de Beze. The homemade vanilla ice cream with frais du bois (wild strawberries) was a special accent point at the end of the meal. It was a little too chilly to eat outside that day, but Jacques chuckled as he told the story that they normally only invite people to dine who are strong enough to lift the dining room table back and forth through the dining room window to the porch.

One of our favorite restaurants in Spain for many years has been the three-star Arzak, where we have been fortunate enough to get to know Juan Mari and his daughter Elena. On our second visit there in 1999, the cellar was out of several red Burgundy wines we had tried to order from the wine list, so I decided to ask if they had any 1968 Vega Sicilia Unico. We had enjoyed a Vega Sicilia Reserva on a prior visit and had heard that the 1968 was one of the greatest bottles ever produced by this legendary Spanish winery. They did have some and agreed to sell us the wine, even though it was not on the list, and we were more than happy to share this 1968 Vega Sicilia with the Arzaks and their staff. While I have also had the great 1962 and 1970 Vega Sicilia Unicos over the years, the 1968 remains for me the definitive example of the greatest, food-friendly Spanish wine I have ever tasted.

On a 1995 trip to Italy, we were surprised to discover that many great French wines were selling for less in Italy than they were in France. At Il Bottaccio di Montignoso on the west coast of Italy, we ordered a 1985 DRC Richebourg and had to wait an hour until the sommelier finally reached the owner at home to see if he was willing to sell us this special bottle. It was delicious, but still needed a few more years to reach its peak (which is the case with many young DRCs). A day later, at what was then a three-star Michelin restaurant outside Milan named Antica Osteria del Ponte, we ordered a 1985 LaTache that was drinking incredibly well even then. To drink two French Burgundies of this quality and value on consecutive nights in Italy is something no longer as readily available.

Le Millesimes in Gevrey Chambertin was a restaurant in the heart of the Côte de Nuits in Burgundy. The quality of the wine cellar was unfortunately too far ahead of its food. It had a Burgundy wine list that was truly the deepest of any restaurant we have ever visited in the world. We took advantage of the opportunity to choose two of the greatest trophy wines of all time—the 1989 Lafon Meursault Perrières and the 1985 Ponsot Clos de la Roche—to drink in the same meal. Unfortunately, this restaurant eventually went bankrupt and had to sell off its magnificent cellar. I never understood why, with such an outstanding wine cellar, Le Millesimes was not better supported by the wine trade or did not become the most popular wine-centric restaurant in all of Burgundy.

A few times in one's life the opportunity occurs to drink a great wine in a setting that makes it even more memorable. We were having lunch at the Hotel la Plages in St. Anne La Palude on the northwest coast of Brittany in April 2005. To accompany a wonderful, fresh Breton lobster, we were able to order the 2000 Coche Dury Meursault Perrieres, which drank perfectly with the lobster because of the depth of flavors that only Coche Dury can produce. It was raining lightly that day, and out of the fog in front of us on the seemingly endless sand beach at low tide came a couple galloping on horseback toward the restaurant. Sitting under a glass-covered roof listening to the raindrops and drinking this perfect white Burgundy, with the unique minerality that the Perrieres vineyard brings to great Meursault wines, was a moment never to be forgotten.

The opportunity to drink Coche Dury is much greater in Europe than in the United States, so we were excited to again have the 2000 Coche Dury Meursault Perrieres at Fat Duck outside London in March 2007. This was a wonderful complement to Heston Blumenthal's innovative snail pudding. To also have a 2002 Coche Dury Volnay and a 1999 Gaja Barbaresco the same night made this a very memorable evening.

We visited Boyer les Crayères in Reims seven times, and always enjoyed whatever Grand Cru vintage Champagne was being offered that month at a retail price. We normally consumed at least three bottles per day with lunch and dinner (as well as what we called tea time), and Gerard Boyer's food was always quite compatible with these glorious Champagnes.

Drinking a DRC wine at a restaurant has now gone well beyond the reach of most consumers (including ourselves). And to get the quality of the three greatest vineyards produced by DRC (Romanée Conti, LaTache, and Richebourg) is always at a tremendous price premium. The DRC wines are usually sold to restaurants and consumers in mixed cases that often include one bottle of Romanée-Conti and a combination of LaTache, Richebourg, Romanée St. Vivant, Grands-Echezeaux, and Echezeaux to fill out the twelve-bottle case. (Pricing of the wines when purchased individually is in the descending order listed above.)

It was assumed that every wine connoisseur and restaurant in the world understands this pecking order. But the possibility that a restaurant would order a mixed case of the great DRC wines and then not know what it had or how to price each individual bottle on its wine list never occurred to me until we visited Edouard Loubet's great restaurant in Lourmarin in April 2004 for a special al fresco Sunday lunch. Upon reading the wine list, it was immediately apparent that they had no idea how to price any of the bottles that they were so obviously proud to offer.

The 2000 Echezeaux was on the list for twice the price of the LaTache, which appeared as the lowest priced wine. LaTache can sell at retail for three to four times the price of the Eche-zeaux. It was all that this Burgundy lover could do to contain himself. I asked the sommelier two different times if he would check with someone whether this was the correct price for the LaTache and both times received a positive answer (I didn't want my bill to double at the end of the meal). I did feel a little guilty about ordering the second bottle of LaTache from this accessible and early-drinking vintage that was still spicy and sexy as only a LaTache can be.

We have had some of our greatest California wine-drink-ing experiences at The French Laundry and its sister restau-rant in New York, Per Se. On one wedding anniversary dinner celebrated at the French Laundry, the 1997 Marcassin from Sonoma's Marcassin Vineyard was extremely memorable, with its beautiful vanilla aftertaste and balanced fruit bouquet. At a special lunch with the Evenstads and my son Todd at Per Se in May 2007, we enjoyed the 2002 Marcassin Vineyard along with a 2002 Groffier Bonnes Mares and the 2002 initial vintage Mono-gram Pinot Noir from Domaine Serene. It seems that American wines are well matched to the cooking of Thomas Keller, and Keller's restaurants always feature a thoughtful list of both domestic and French choices.

One of our most bizarre wine and food evenings was spent at Gilt in New York City with the eccentric and talented chef Paul Liebrandt, who is now cooking at Corton with great suc-cess and two Michelin stars. Even though a plane delay made us an hour late to the restaurant, they still agreed to serve us the full tasting menu starting at 10:00 P.M. Liebrandt's food is extremely creative and flavorful, and he was really on that night. A 1996 Roumier Bonnes Mares caught my eye at a price below retail. For the white, we selected a simple 2000 Michel Coutoux Meursault Charmes, a vintage between the two great white Burgundy years (1996 and 2002) I was enjoying a great deal. The wine was obviously corked with no bouquet and completely lacking in fruit.

The sommelier displayed a condescending attitude, and it immediately became obvious that he did not regard us as valued customers. He refused to taste the wine, even when we asked him to do so. He reluctantly took it back after some polite discussion, and we then selected a different white wine so as not to put ourselves through this hassle again.

When we observed the sommelier quietly tasting the wine in the corner some time later, we asked him what he thought. His reply was consistent with his prior attitude: "I think I'm really going to enjoy this bottle of wine later tonight." Such behavior by a New York City sommelier in a fine-dining restaurant was hard to believe. The accent point of the evening was Liebrandt appearing at the top of the stairs in a fog of dry ice being blown out of his elevated kitchen with his arms held up high (Olympian like).

Corks can present a problem. We have had several white Burgundies from the 1996 vintage go bad over the years because of the corks. We experienced this firsthand at Rochat's wonderful three-star restaurant outside Lausanne, Switzerland, when two straight bottles of 1996 Comte de Lafon Clos de Barre were undrinkable, leading us to shift to another wine selection. The restaurant handled it beautifully, and I have so much respect for the way the sommelier and the maître d' put our interests first.

With all of these great wine experiences, is it possible to point out one meal where everything seemed to come together? The greatest wine meal of my life was certainly on the day of my sixtieth birthday at Michel Bras. I had brought a magnum of 1945 Mouton Rothschild to share with our two sons and two chefs from Minneapolis, Vincent Francoual and Ferris Shiffer, as well as Vincent's wife Joanne. To drink a 1993 Lafon Meursault Perrieres, a 1945 Mouton Rothschild, the legendary 1988 Henri Jayer Cros Parantoux, and top it all off with a 1975 La Tour Blanche Sauterne made me declare that night that I never again had to celebrate another birthday.

🍴

CHAPTER 16

Establishing Wine Traditions and the Joy of Sharing

WINE TRADITIONS CAN MAKE HOLIDAYS MEMORABLE AS WELL. We started drinking Bouchard Pere's Vigne d'Enfant Jésus in 1975 at our first Christmas dinner after we moved to Minnesota. The 1969 vintage was superb, and this lighter Cote de Beaune red Burgundy from the Grèves region is a nice complement to all the rich foods we consume at Christmas. A picture of the Christ child appears on the label, which seems quite appropriate to enjoy on Christmas Day (and occasionally on Easter). I have been regularly collecting many of the great red Burgundy vintages of this wine (1993, 1996, 1999, 2002, 2005) to be able to drink one every year that has aged ten years or more.

Since 1994, we have instituted an annual port tasting evening with our friends Steve and Martha O'Hara, and more recently have included chef Ferris Shiffer, and friends Howard Stacker and Tillie Kitzenberg. We always share several special wines out of our cellars, but a bottle of port is selected to be the featured star of the evening, along with several kinds of English Stilton cheese. Although we have had many memorable ports on these cold Minnesota January and February evenings, a 1912 Croft and one special 1945 Quinta do Noval Nacional stand out as the greatest ones we have ever tasted. The depth of fruit, lingering aftertaste, and the complexity of flavors provide another level of enjoyment in these incredible aged, vintage ports.

I must include a story that will seem truly ironic after all these memorable trophy-wine adventures over the years. I have been quite fortunate to have had many hundreds of the greatest Bordeauxs and Burgundies in my life and can still remember distinctly how most of them tasted and how they enhanced a particular meal. Our visits to California, Spain, and Italy have included many of the legendary local wines from these areas as well. Yet in the fall of 1967, before we began studying about wines or eating more regularly at gourmet restaurants, I took Sue (who was my fiancée at that time) to a modest restaurant on the Upper East Side of New York City. While listening to a flamenco guitarist (I don't remember why I chose this place) and knowing absolutely nothing about wines at the time, I ordered a sweet French Sauterne with the main meat course. This is because of what I recalled my father had done many years before in Paris when I was fifteen years old. I can only look back on this evening in New York with amusement at what has since come to pass in our wine experiences.

Wine collecting is really a simple hobby. The trick is to find wines that meet your individual taste and enjoy them regularly as your "house wines." If it brings enjoyment to drink only a white or red wine with a meal, who is to say this is not acceptable and proper. And no one can ever know more than a small part of what there is to learn about the various wines from around the world. Even the best wine connoisseurs can be fooled in blind tastings. Experts who drink red and white wines at the same temperature from a black glass can be challenged to even distinguish whether a wine is white or red. I'm serious! So, our eyes and pre-knowledge of what we are drinking can be an important influence in how we judge and even enjoy a wine.

The likely health benefits of wine are an encouraging exclamation point to this chapter. Recent scientific studies have shown that drinking half a glass of red wine a day (the polyphenol compounds found in tannins make it the best type of alcohol) can add up to five years to one's average life expectancy. Lower cardiovascular mortality is a direct effect from the resulting increase in good cholesterol and a reduction in the platelet clumping that forms clots.

I respect that wine is a living thing in the bottle. Yet a wine can only be as good as the quality of its grapes. And drinking great wine with great food, while an intimate experience, also needs to be discussed if it is to be fully enjoyed. These stimulating and often intense conversations (with occasional differences of opinion) are an important part of providing many interesting memories.

My wine hero will always be André Simon, the founder of the International Wine and Food Society and a highly respected wine critic in his time. He knew how to manage his wine collection and understood the real joy that comes from sharing. Simon died with only three bottles left in his cellar.

PART III

Megatrends: Celebrity Chefs, Healthier Food, and Bolder Flavors

℣◎℣

CHAPTER 17
The Era of Celebrity Chefs

THE GREATEST CONTRIBUTIONS OF CELEBRITY CHEFS MAY HAVE been to change people's expectations about fine dining and to get them more interested in food as a hobby. For some chefs, cooking appears to have become a celebrity sport. While these television chefs are often encouraged to make their cooking demonstrations and contests take on a circus atmosphere, they do raise awareness of the whole food experience as both educational and fun. Even adults and children who are not interested in gourmet food love watching The Food Channel and shows like *Top Chef* or *Iron Chef*. Being a working chef in a kitchen is a tough, grinding avocation, however, and not at all like it is portrayed on television.

Celebrity chefs do provide real entertainment for a growing number of people. Many television viewers enjoy food with little knowledge of the technical aspects of cooking. Watching these shows, however, will not expose them to the signature dishes these chefs are capable of preparing in their own restaurants.

The standards by which these shows are often judged, and the absurd combinations of food ingredients that must be used in a course, provide results far removed from what one might call great cooking. The shows are more likely to focus on the often bizarre personalities of the chef contestants, and may even encourage conflicts to generate viewer interest. By challenging the creativity of top-level chefs to produce unusual dishes that they would never serve in their own restaurants, these television shows seem to be creating a different form of reality television.

With the added dimension of time limits, these shows have for me the entertainment value of a horse race. When subjective judging, often by semi-knowledgeable non-chefs is considered, we are left with no more credibility than food blogs where "everyone is an expert." The results never seem to achieve great cooking, and they only dumb down what these chefs are capable of doing. It is not surprising that (with the exception of *Iron Chef*), the most talented chefs never choose to cook on these shows.

A number of the more prominent, business-oriented celebrity chefs have opened multiple restaurants in various food capitals of the world including Paris, London, New York, Tokyo, and Las Vegas. They are regularly gone from their "home kitchens" to try to duplicate the recipes and purveyor sources (wherever possible) in these other locations to ensure successful openings and ongoing success. Their self-promotion often includes publishing cookbooks and even selling frozen products in grocery stores.

Within this group of celebrity chefs, several high-profile personalities have taken "branding" to a new level. Before the recession in 2009, New York-based Jean-Georges Vongerichten was said to be planning to open up as many as fifty more restaurants over the next five years in addition to the twenty-seven he had already launched worldwide. Among the other top-branded chefs, Los Angeles-based Wolfgang Puck has opened ninety-two restaurants including his Wolfgang Puck Expresses; and London-based Gordon Ramsay has twenty-three restaurants, which include both high-end operations and casual gastro pubs. The Frenchman Alain Ducasse has twenty-four restaurants while Nobu Matsuhisa has enjoyed great success at expanding his Los Angeles flagship Japanese restaurant to include more than thirty-one restaurants around the world. While some of these chefs' restaurants will continue to close and new restaurant openings may be deferred, the sheer numbers of these chef empires is nevertheless astounding.

One result of these celebrity chefs spending less time in their kitchens is the potentially adverse impact on not only the quality of the food being served, but on their time for and interest in developing new menu ideas. With these external distractions, the chefs may not be achieving the same degree of ongoing creativity that made them so successful in the first place. And because running a restaurant as a successful business also requires an increasing emphasis on cost controls, this can eventually begin to impact the quality of the ingredients purchased as cooking becomes much less a labor of love.

Celebrity chefs increasingly see themselves in the business of entertaining the customer. This can subtly change the emphasis from focusing on what is great food to what is new and glamorous. The old-school way of thinking that the chef belongs in his kitchen training his staff and being totally dedicated to his cooking is becoming less evident in this current generation of young chefs, who seem to be much more interested in achieving recognition and chasing the big dollars.

One of the other subtle impacts of gourmet cooking going corporate with multiple locations has been that some of the best and brightest young chefs starting their careers are now being hired to cook the celebrity chefs' recipes in these new locations, rather than developing their own unique regional cuisines in a local neighborhood restaurant. And because running a restaurant is so demanding and opening one involves real financial risk, some chefs eventually opt for a more predictable daily routine and stable employment, often with fewer hours. This might include becoming a hotel or country club chef to achieve a better work/life balance, and with it may come, for some, a dumbing down of opportunities to develop more creative food offerings.

꒰◎꒱

CHAPTER 18

Organic Food and Eating Healthy

WHILE THIS TREND TO HIGH-VISIBILITY, MULTIPLE-LOCATION celebrity restaurants seems inevitable, several parallel trends may help neighborhood chefs survive—and even thrive—amidst this increasingly difficult competition. The organic food movement, emphasizing sustainable, local ingredients, provides neighborhood chefs an exciting way to distinguish themselves through their menu offerings, while also developing a highly loyal group of supporters who share this more health-conscious approach as a priority. While the organic movement started out focusing on fresh produce, it has expanded to include the full variety of foods including meats, eggs, and fish, with an emphasis on using sustainable, locally produced sources whenever possible.

Mark Bittman, writing for the *New York Times*, notes that the strict meaning of true organic is that it is free of synthetic substances, contains no antibiotics or hormones, has not been irradiated or fertilized, was raised without the use of conventional pesticides, and contains no genetically modified ingredients. The enabling registration and accompanying regulations around organic foods currently say nothing, however, about food safety, the nutritional value of the food, or whether the animals involved have been raised humanely.

Bittman points out that about 30% of Americans buy organic food at least occasionally. While sales of organic foods have doubled over the last decade, ever since the federal government began certifying food as "organic," they still amount to slightly less than 3% of all foods sold, which is hardly a significant impact. Many major corporations have been jumping into the organic food business and are now responsible for at least 25% of all organic foods on the market, or as much as 40% if only processed organic foods are counted.

The sustainable, organic movement offers chefs the chance to develop more flavorful foods and distinguish themselves by listing their artisan purveyors on their menus. This also allows them to take proper credit for helping the environment by buying locally produced products, which can minimize transportation costs. Sustainable seafood, which prevents over-fishing and emphasizes the superior flavor of wild, live-caught fish, is another growing trend. Open-water aquaculture farms are employing water monitoring systems and sustainable sources for feeding the fish, and utilizing "harvest-to-order" methods to cut waste.

Organic milk, cheese, butter, eggs, juice, and soy milk are generally believed to have a superior taste and higher nutritional value. Because of the absence of toxins, fresh produce is being grown in a way that ensures vitality and returns nutrients to the soil, and by eliminating the use of toxic pesticides and herbicides, the surrounding air and water can be safer from pollutants.

For the past thirty years, subsidies in the USDA Farm Bill have artificially held down grain prices and kept food costs lower than they otherwise might have been. The result has been an explosion in high yields of corn and soy, so by-products such as high fructose corn syrup used for sweetening soft drinks, cheap feed for livestock, and hydrogenated oils (which can produce health hazards) have been made more available at reasonable prices. Surpluses of corn and soy have driven business decisions to find uses for these lower-cost products in the mass consumption markets such as fast-food restaurants and processed foods. Not surprisingly, fresh produce has remained relatively more expensive.

It is estimated that food prices would go up over thirty percent if fertilizer and other farm chemicals were not used to boost production and prevent diseases. At the same time, fertilizer made from synthetic nitrogen (which depends on natural gas) is becoming increasingly more expensive. Even more importantly, the fresh water supply is becoming limited in the quantities required; farming uses 75% of all fresh water consumption in the United States today. Because it is so dependent on these two elements, high-volume agriculture may be reaching a flex point from which it will not be able to increase production. As the fuels used for transporting food and making fertilizer are become dramatically more expensive, modern, high-volume agriculture may face a crisis in its own sustainability. Seasonal foods that do not need to be transported long distances need to become an increasing part of any economic solution.

As *Saveur* magazine noted, the USDA Farm Bill 2007 included—for the first time—some funds "to encourage farmers to go organic, build local food systems, promote farmers' markets, and bring more fruits and vegetables into the schools, while encouraging school lunch programs to buy from local farmers." Instead of subsidizing the least healthful calories in the supermarket (in the form of processed foods with added fats and sugars), some emphasis is finally being placed on growing the "real food" that consumers are demanding—for better flavor and their own well-being. Yet the government continues to pay about $7.5 billion in farm subsidies for growing grains and soybeans compared with only $15 million dollars for the programs supporting organic and local foods.

The farmers who practice sustainable farming currently operate on such a small scale that some can't even afford the inspections and paperwork required to be certified organic by the government, while others believe that certification isn't meaningful enough to warrant spending the time and money to get it. Unfortunately, many people who wish to buy fresh local or organic foods cannot afford to do so, so we are still a long way away from providing ourselves—and the world—with a significant amount of organic foods.

From both a health and nutrition perspective, the ability to provide healthier school breakfasts and lunches would seem to be a thoughtful focus for government funds. But in a recession, increasing the federal dollars available for child nutrition, and conservation programs that reward farmers for protecting the environment with sustainable farming methods as well as help farmers convert to grass-fed beef, becomes an even more difficult sell. When the total costs of eating healthier foods take into account potential savings on medical bills, however, clear benefits exist from shifting eating habits away from corn-fed animal products and highly processed foods to plant products and what is called "real food."

When British chef Jamie Oliver began a mission to ban junk food in the English school lunch program in an attempt to get children to eat fresher, more nutritious food, he ran into several serious challenges. Even presenting clear evidence that food affects health; obesity; and children's behaviors, moods, and ability to concentrate in school, was not enough to persuade many parents to actively support the program. Cooks in school pilot programs were trained to offer healthy meals that also tasted good, but many parents did not believe their children would finish the full lunch menu and were reluctant to pay for food that might not be eaten. What's more, those students whose family's economic situation made them eligible for subsidized or free meals often did not want to be identified as "needy" by their peers.

The result of this thoughtful experiment was that meals brought from home actually increased during this time for these economic and social reasons, and unfortunately, the parents' food selections in these lunch boxes usually did not meet Oliver's more nutritional, health-oriented suggestions.

The politics of food dictates that high levels of food production will continue to be needed to prevent starvation in countries with high populations. High-cost organic foods will continue to be considered a luxury unless the overall impact on health costs is somehow factored into consideration. Most people can only afford to spend a certain portion of their budget on food, so for many people food will never be a luxury purchase but will remain primarily a means to stave off hunger. Legislators are only starting to become more willing to focus on the production of healthier foods as a means of providing a basis for long-term well-being.

Dan Barber of the Blue Hill at Stone Barns restaurant in Westchester County, New York, has set a great example as one of the first chefs to raise all his own fresh vegetables and many of his meat products (including the pigs) on the restaurant property itself. He is also developing a full-time dairy operation that will provide milk from grass-fed animals for cheese. His high-quality, organically grown vegetables have up to 40% more nutrients than their chemical-fed counterparts and are noticeably more delicious. The animals raised on his pastureland produce meat containing more beta-carotene and three times as much conjugated linoleic acid (CLA), which has been shown in animal studies to help reduce the risk of cancer (when compared to consuming corn-fed animals). Savvy, enlightened chefs are increasingly seeking out foods that offer these better flavors, health benefits, and nutritional value.

Barber has also been a trendsetter in understanding the synergistic relationship between plants and animals. Writing in a May 11, 2008, *New York Times* op-ed, Barber pointed out that, "A dairy farm can provide manure for a neighboring potato farm...which can in turn offer potato scraps as extra food for the herd. When crops and livestock are judiciously mated, agriculture wisely mimics nature." Barber is an important leader in challenging other chefs to establish similar food systems that produce this more flavorful food.

In addition to supporting fresh, local food (which also costs less to transport), Barber advocates a system of "regional farm networks each suited to the food it can grow best." These regional systems will work only if there is enough small-scale farming going on to make them viable "which in turn requires more people on the farm." This means rethinking "how we educate the people who will grow our food."

Barber understands the power of chefs and those who take healthy food seriously to be able to influence our agricultural future. This requires moving away from a "bigger is better" farming style that has been justified on the basis of feeding more people but is not producing any really delicious food. He emphasizes that chefs and foodies must be the ones to demand great cooking that produces fresh flavors and good nutrition, since "the future belongs to the gourmet."

Our meal at Stone Barns was noticeably dedicated to presenting fresh flavors in every course. Similar to what we experienced at Alice Waters' organic restaurant in Berkeley several years before, the natural, fresh flavors were showcased without any strong sauces or oils competing. Simplicity was Barber's theme in the salad and dessert, and the vegetables took equal billing with the meat for the main course.

In many cities and towns throughout France, shopping at a local market that offers a variety of fresh foods has, for centuries, defined the social fabric of people's daily lives. The impact of seeing a freshly caught, ten-pound fish on shaved ice, a whole golden Bresse chicken with its feet and head still on, or bright red and white radishes in a bunch becomes as artistic as a still life painting. The people in the stalls are also often colorful characters, with their typical regional clothing and hats adding to this visual canvas. From the great markets like Aix-en-Provence to traveling markets serving smaller towns once a week, the dedicated artisans selling their fresh unpasteurized cheeses and farm fresh meats, fish, vegetables, fruit, eggs, spices, and flowers present a kaleidoscope of colors and smells, as well as a way of life in shopping daily for fresh ingredients. These healthier food offerings are a primary reason the Europeans have the advantage in the way they eat versus their more obese US counterparts.

French chefs obviously rely on such sources for most of their fresh ingredients, which is why daily pilgrimages to local and regional markets are considered necessary, even for the great restaurants. In the United States, the farmer's market in Union Square in New York City and the Saturday morning market outside the Ferry Building in San Francisco have become increasingly essential parts of the organic food movement in those cities for chefs and consumers alike.

Whereas obesity is not directly a chef's problem, it is a subject that at some point must be addressed by everyone who can have an influence and be part of the solution. Overeating puts oxidative stress on the brain, while eating well has been demonstrated to be the key to a healthy brain. Almost half of America's adults are now overweight, and the trend is moving in the wrong direction. Fat is flavor, and Americans have become so hooked on high-fat fast food that many are choosing it for most of their regular meals. Procuring meals from these highly promoted "production line restaurants" by parents too busy to cook at home is taking its toll. Even in gourmet restaurants, the perception exists that large portions should accompany the higher prices. Recent trends to multiple courses with small plates, or smaller-portioned servings at reduced prices, offer much healthier solutions.

In addition to the growing crisis brought on by an overweight dining population, a related issue is whether the food we are consuming is actually healthy to eat. When cattle are being fed corn rather than their natural food (which is grass), many animals have to be aggressively medicated to keep them from getting sick. This directly impacts how human beings are affected when they eat this "medicated" food, since it can exacerbate such chronic illnesses as diabetes and arthritis. While less tender, grass-fed beef is also more flavorful and far healthier than corn- or bonemeal-fed beef, which has the unfortunate effect of raising our omega-6 fatty acids and lowering the beneficial omega-3 fatty acids. Free-range chickens that feed on bugs and insects are also healthier to eat and usually taste better as well.

Chefs remain in control of another critical aspect of healthy food: the cooking oils they use. A common notion exists that saturated fats can cause heart attacks, and legislators have even tried to ban them through legislation. But weren't many of these same saturated fat foods and oils being consumed for centuries before the current obesity crisis and other health problems arose?

Many chefs and nutritionists strongly believe that consuming saturated animal fats in moderation are really not all that harmful. Olive oil, butter from pasture-raised cows, duck fat, lard, canola, and cold-pressed sunflower oil are among the most healthy saturated fats. Polyunsaturated oils made from corn or soy are far more dangerous because they can become rancid (since they are less stable at high temperatures). In fact, almost any cooking oil that is used continuously in a deep fat fryer for a long enough time will produce dangerous trans fats, which pose the biggest threat to human kidneys and livers.

Trans fat can be created by pumping hydrogen into liquid oil at a high temperature. This process (known as a partial hydrogenation) is frequently used to prolong shelf life, improve the appearance of packaged foods, help these foods withstand high cooking temperatures, and, in principle, make the food crisper and tastier. Unfortunately, trans fats also increase the low-density lipoproteins found in the bad cholesterol, which directly increases the probability of heart disease. The focus of any legislation would seem to be better directed at discontinuing use of those oils, margarines, and shortenings containing the unhealthy trans fats, which contribute significantly to obesity.

The *Economist* did an in-depth study recently on the impact of food on human behavior. Research reported on the positive benefits of vitamin D and omega-3 fatty acids found in oily fish like salmon, as well as in walnuts and kiwi fruit. In places where people consume large quantities of fish (such as Okinawa), a lower rate of mental disorders has been documented. Eating healthy also requires getting a better balance of vitamin D, which is necessary for calcium absorption both from the intestines and into bone. When vitamin D is lacking in diets of the elderly, it can lead to osteoporosis, fractures, and muscle weakness; it has also been implicated in depression, common colds, and autoimmune diseases including multiple sclerosis and cardiovascular diseases. The high amounts of saturated fatty acids found in deep-fried foods and butter have been shown to adversely affect cognitive skills. Mark Bittman notes it is estimated that cutting the high sodium content found in most processed foods could eventually save up to one hundred thousand lives a year.

Pregnant women increasingly understand the importance of embracing a diet with a mix of foods that ensure greater health in their unborn children and have a direct impact on gene development. Dense foods like grains usually work particularly well for pregnant women, growing children, and those recovering from serious injuries. Folic acid found in spinach and orange juice can help ward off the cognitive decline that accompanies aging. Eating more antioxidants (found in nuts, leafy green vegetables, and fruits such as blueberries) can slow down the effects of aging. Such foods have directly reduced oxidation damage in tests on rodents, and possibly increased their ability to learn and retain memories. With Alzheimers disease impacting the short-term memory of the brain, it is interesting to note that in India, Alzheimers is rare. The natives there eat a lot of cumin.

Becoming a vegetarian does not necessarily appear to be a solution for achieving better health. Man evolved as an omnivore with jaws, teeth, and a digestive tract to consume meat. Maintaining good health has long meant getting enough critical amino acids from B12, found primarily in meat. Dedicated vegetarians and vegans do not achieve any moral high ground if their health suffers from a lack of B12 and iron. It is hard to justify the appearance of some vegetarians with the grey skin under their eyes and an obvious lack of energy, no matter what level of empathy they have for the plight of animals. By keeping an open mind, the non vegan vegetarians can benefit from egg whites, which contain an important source of high-quality protein, while the yolks provide an absorbable iron source that is good for combating cataracts and muscular degeneration.

Despite numerous economic challenges, eating healthy is an increasingly popular lifestyle that, for many, will no longer be compromised. Diners who can afford it are supporting the narrow but growing cadre of chefs who choose to distinguish themselves by serving menus that primarily feature organic food using local, sustainable sources. Freshness and natural flavors are now being demanded as an integral part of some consumer's lifestyles. Increasingly, these diners may choose to ignore fast food and bargain-priced dining chains built on high-fat and high-carbohydrate choices. Knowledgeable foodies also understand the importance of strongly supporting those local neighborhood chefs who are thoughtfully choosing natural ingredients.

⑨

CHAPTER 19
Specialty Meats and Comfort Food

THE HIGH END OF THE CONSUMER SPECTRUM IS ACQUIRING A taste for Japanese Kobe beef and more recently US-produced Wagyu beef, which is a crossbreed of Kobe and Angus cattle. The black Tajíma-ushi breed in Japan is extremely flavorful, tender, and well-marbled, due to the fact that it is fed a diet of beer (and sake) as well as an expensive grain fodder. The cattle are even massaged and brushed on a regular basis. The Wagyu beef in the United States is generally fed a less expensive diet of grass and grain.

Pork products have also been enjoying a renaissance with the Berkshire breed that dates back 300 years to herds at the House of Windsor in England. This can provide pork of exceptional taste and tenderness. In addition, the curly-haired Mangalitsa pigs of Hungary are also making a comeback and sell for three dollars a pound more than the Berkshire pork. Mangalitsa is well-marbled, and the fat seems to dissolve on the tongue; it is softer and creamier, akin to Wagyu beef. The Mangalitsas are particularly popular in Spain where they become ham and other cured meats, and recently they are being raised on farms in the United States as well.

In what is becoming a pork revolution, chefs are increasingly cooking all parts of the pig. At Paul Kahan's Publican restaurant in Chicago, pork is the star and comes in the form of tenderloin, sausage, rillettes, crispy pig ears, and pork rinds served in a cone. The cult following for the over-the-top Au Pied du Cochon in Montreal enjoys Martin Picard's pig's trotter and other creative forms of pork dishes, along with his "Duck in a Can" and poutine served with foie gras and foie gras gravy on the French fries. Many chefs are designing entire menus around bacon, which is so delicious when cooked correctly that it can be a wonderful accompaniment in soups, salads, and even desserts such as crème brûlée.

Many talented chefs around the world have been emphasizing less expensive comfort food, which has become a significant dining trend during the recent recession. The resurgence in popularity of artisan pizzas, hamburgers served with different toppings, macaroni and cheese, gourmet hot dogs, barbequed ribs, and rotisserie chickens, however, does not contribute to any healthy food trend. Steakhouses with their high-fat offerings seem to do well in all economic times. Even cheaper cuts of fatty meat are being well-received when they are cooked sous vide (under vacuum) to make the texture more tender and the flavors more concentrated.

This comfort food trend has even been recognized in recent years in the annual James Beard awards, where David Chang of Momofuku Noodle Bar and Momofuku Ssäm Bar in New York City (which offer high-fat pork buns and pork noodle dishes) won the James Beard "Rising Star Chef" and "Outstanding Restaurant in New York City" respectively in back-to-back years. His restaurants have become wildly popular and represent a seismic shift away from the high-end gourmet restaurants long selected for these prestigious Beard awards. Simple comfort food, more intense flavors, less pretense, and casual atmosphere are all in strong demand today. People increasingly enjoy the informality of sitting at counters to view the chefs in open kitchens and interact with the bartenders and waiters.

ïↀï

CHAPTER 20
Peppers and Bolder Flavors

BOLDER FLAVORS THROUGH PEPPERS AND SPICES ARE GOING to be an increasingly important part of cooking in the future. It is important to have some knowledge about the wide variety of spices (long used as staples in many ethnic dishes) now increasingly used in gourmet cooking. The New York three-star chef Jean Georges Vongerichten has been noticeably putting more heat in his cooking recently, and Eric Ripert of Le Bernardin has used spices to accent his fish dishes for many years.

People who are naturally attracted to spice may feel it makes their food more exciting. Spices tend to mask the nuances of great wines, however, which is why spicier wines such as Zinfandel, Gewürztraminer, Amarone, and the bolder Rhônes are often the best matches for spicy food. As people build up a tolerance to increasingly hotter flavors, more subtly flavored classical French dishes may seem less appealing to their palates. We experienced this for a time when we lived in Singapore, where a steady diet of the hotter Indian, Malaysian, and Schezuan food started to make our European meals seem bland by comparison.

The growing influence of street food on both high-end cooking and fast-food menus cannot be underestimated. Cravings for these spicier flavors has focused greater attention on the capsaicin levels of various peppers that are increasingly being used in ethnic and new-wave gourmet cooking.

Capsaicin itself is odorless and flavorless and is primarily found in a pepper's seeds and ribs (veins). Even a modest dose of this natural heat-causing component can produce sweat, tears, and a quickening of the pulse. It floods the bloodstream with endorphins, which is the closest thing to morphine that the body can produce. Hot chiles are being used not only in main courses but also in unexpected applications, such as cocktails and even chocolate, to satisfy the cravings of a whole generation becoming increasingly tolerant to higher levels of capsaicin.

The relative heat of these peppers is now measured in ranges of Scoville heat units (SHUS). Traditionally, habanero (Bolivian, chocolate, Peruvian, and red types exist) and Scotch bonnet peppers have been at the top of the "heat scale" at 100,000 to 300,000 SHUS. However, the Dorset Naga (1,600,000 SHUS) and the Naga Jolokia (over 1,000,000 SHUS) peppers found in northeast India, Bangladesh, and Sri Lanka are now the hottest ever recorded by the *Guinness Book of Records*; they are so intolerable to most humans that they can be painful even to the touch. (Pure capsaicin measures 16,000,000 SHUS.)

A large number of pepper varieties now exist, and their origins and food applications could fill an entire book. Some of the more popular peppers will be highlighted here. Bell peppers have no SHUS. The popular poblano pepper (500 to 2,500 SHUS) is spicier than a bell pepper but mild enough to be used in sauces, salsas, stuffing mixes, and chile rellenos. The dried version of poblano is an ancho chile. It is interesting to note that flavor will vary depending on whether the pepper used is fresh, dried, pickled, or smoked.

Habanero peppers (100,000 to 300,000 SHUS) are most often used in Caribbean cooking, while Mexican cooking uses jalapeños (8,000 SHUS). The extra-hot African Bird's Eye peppers (100,000 to 350,000 SHUS) are found primarily in Thai cooking. Cayenne (30,000 SHUS) peppers are medium-hot, and are often found in Cajun gumbos and Mexican sauces; they can even be strung together as a colorful decoration. Cayenne peppers also have proven to burn extra calories when ingested with or after a meal.

Evidence is growing that capsaicin can have wonderful health benefits in killing prostate cancer cells, repressing joint pain, blocking pro-inflammatory chain reactions in the bloodstream, reducing nerve fiber swelling in the brain, and even promoting fat oxidation. It is not surprising that pills containing capsaicin are being used as vitamin and weight-loss supplements. Capsaicin can also block the pain of arthritis and "help patients with multiple sclerosis, amputees and people undergoing therapy," according to a December 2008 *Economist* article.

Hot peppers can induce a craving, but have not been proven to be addictive. Whereas a large dose of capsaicin can incapacitate a person, there is no evidence that any permanent physical damage or stripping away of the stomach lining will result. Most people are not aware that there are more nerve endings in our digestive tract than in the human brain, so our bodies are extremely sensitive to the foods being ingested.

Cooks are branching out dramatically from using just the basic salt, black pepper, garlic, ginger, and wasabi (Japanese horseradish) flavorings that are so wonderful in many ethnic dishes. Soy sauce (which was invented in China) is the salty liquid used primarily in Japanese and South Asian cooking and as a seasoning at the table; it is finding increasing acceptance in the United States. The best soy sauce is made with naturally fermented soybeans, roasted grains (such as wheat), yeast and other related microorganisms, plus water and salt.

Harissa, used originally in Algerian and Tunisian recipes, is a garlicky paste made from red chiles and incorporates the moderately hot Mexican guajillo chiles (2,500 to 8,000 SHUS). These dark, leathery, reddish-brown peppers are dried by toasting, then salt and olive oil are added to form the paste (which also incorporates mint and onions in some versions). It is used increasingly by chefs as a condiment in their cooking and continues to be a key ingredient in such traditional North African dishes as goat, lamb, red lentil soup, and the chickpea soup often eaten for breakfast.

American-made Srichacha is a spicy, red jalapeño pepper sauce that includes garlic powder, sugar, salt, and vinegar. The bottle with the rooster on it is on the table at most Vietnamese restaurants, to be added to traditional dishes such as pho (soup) and the green papaya salad. Srichacha is now being used like ketchup by chefs all over the world to add bolder flavors to many foods, including Jean-Georges' rice-cracker-crusted tuna.

Hoisin, a soy-based Chinese dipping sauce made from soybean paste, garlic, vinegar, and chile peppers, is often used on barbequed meats and Peking duck. Several versions of this sweet and spicy, reddish-brown sauce include other ingredients such as peanut sauce, honey, molasses, white vinegar, sesame oil, and a hot pepper sauce. Kecap Manis is a sweet, thick soy sauce with garlic and star anise that is sweetened with palm sugar and is used as a condiment and marinade in Indonesian cooking. Thai red curry paste mixes Arbol chiles (15,000–30,000 SHUS) with coriander, cumin, garlic, shallots, cilantro, and lemongrass to accent chicken and fish dishes, marinate steak, and provide the basis for chicken curries enriched with coconut milk. These narrow, curved, bright red chiles (called "bird's beak" or "rat's tail" in Mexico), add a natural grassy flavor to dishes, and in pod form can flavor oils and vinegars.

Even the leaves of the chile pepper plant can be cooked and served as a vegetable. These are frequently used in chicken soup recipes in the Philippines and Japan. In Korea, the leaves are one of the primary flavorings in kimchi, the pickled vegetables made from cabbage, radishes, and cucumbers.

Fermented fish sauce is used like soy sauce and salt as the basic staple in Thai cooking. The unique flavor of the juice from the flesh of the fish is extracted during prolonged salting and fermentation, which also provides its translucent reddish-golden brown color. It provides a basic accent to Thai curries, salads, and noodle dishes, as well as marinades for fish and meat.

Another spicy sauce is the Tabasco brand pepper sauce made from the red tabasco (20,000 to 50,000 SHUS) or red Amazon peppers (capsicum frutescens) to which vinegar and salt are added. Tabasco has become the world's best selling chile-based condiment, and several additional chile sauces (an extra-hot version using habanero peppers, a mild green jalapeño version, and a smoked chipotle option) have been introduced to meet a variety of palates.

Slightly different versions of Worchestershire sauce are made in the United States and England and are used to provide an accent to meat dishes. Both utilize tamarind (the sweet, fruit pulp pod from the tamarind tree, usually from India) as the basic ingredient. The US version features vinegar, molasses, corn syrup, anchovies, onions, garlic salt, cloves, and a chile pepper extract. The English version (Lea & Perrins) also incorporates anchovies, onions, garlic, sugar, and malt and spirit vinegars. Tamarind is also a basic ingredient of Jamaican Pickapeppa sauce.

The Puerto Rican soffrito incorporates ají dulce chiles (30,000 to 50,000 SHUs) with green peppers, onions, garlic, and herbs to product a piquant green paste used in soups, stews, and traditional dishes such as rice with pigeon peas. It is also a delicious marinade for meat and adds zest to many sauces. The Peruvian ají pepper ripens to a bright yellow; it has a lemony flavor when served fresh, and has more of a banana flavor when dried.

Chefs are increasingly using these peppers and prepared seasonings in their foams and sauces to accent nontraditional dishes, and in moderation they do not detract from the meat or fish but provide an interesting aftertaste to a course. As people become more sophisticated about the peppers they consume, it is possible that their palates might become less discerning and more one-dimensional if they simply begin craving more and more heat!

⚟◉⚟

CHAPTER 21

Future Trends—The Dining Revolution Continues

SO WHAT WILL OUR FOOD EXPERIENCES AND PRIORITIES BE twenty years from now? Gourmet cooking undoubtedly will still be just as demanding a profession. A chef's ability to offer new and creative courses using unique but compatible combinations of ingredients and to properly cook meat or fish will continue to define his or her reputation. People will be making their dining choices based more and more on the reputation of the chef and on their most recent experience at restaurants, not just on some general impression of a restaurant's menu or atmosphere (as was the case twenty years ago). Most chefs will go into their profession with idealistic expectations about what they can accomplish, but many will continue to compromise their goals when faced with the realities of making a living, the hard work involved, and the influence of their families on quality of life considerations (as they seek to ensure a more balanced lifestyle that includes some outside interests).

Cooking schools will continue to be in strong demand (even for college graduates). Teaching about healthy foods and emphasizing healthy eating will become a more integral part of the curriculum at cooking schools. It will be the right-brained, artistic, and creative types still looking for a career niche who will continue to gravitate to the chef profession for an opportunity to fully express their passions. Chefs will increasingly emphasize healthy food choices in their ingredients and cooking, supported to a greater extent by doctors who are demanding more comprehensive nutrition courses in medical schools so doctors better understand the health factors.

The days of successful, self-taught chefs may be limited, as cooking school diplomas will become a more important prerequisite for getting jobs in the kitchens of the best-known chefs. When starting one's own restaurant, the risks of success will be much higher due to increasing competition and higher levels of expectations by diners. Cooking schools must expose the next generation of chefs not only to basic cooking techniques but to the economics of a restaurant; future chefs will need to learn prudent purchasing and food cost management, as well as have a basic understanding of how to monitor the critical revenues-per-labor-hour measurement.

Multiple cuisine choices are now available in every country, with the popularity of experiencing different international cuisines continuing to grow among each new generation. Even serious food countries such as France and Japan will have to live with the ongoing incursion of fast-food restaurants. Classic Chinese and Japanese cuisines are likely to be increasingly embraced globally, now reinforced by the Michelin Guide ratings for those countries (which are followed closely by foodies worldwide).

Innovations may include new textures, continuing experiments with the impact of temperatures on taste, and more flavorful fat and carbohydrate substitutes available not only in restaurants but in grocery stores and health food stores as well. Recognizing the dramatic influence of chefs such as Ferran Adrià at elBulli, the genie is out of the bottle, and cooking will never again be quite the same. Food chemistry will attract increasing research attention to deconstructing classic dishes into their individual elements in ways that are exciting and intellectually stimulating. Spending an entire evening eating multiple courses will continue to grow in importance as a widely accepted form of recreation.

To feed the world, awareness about—and production of—organic soybeans and other healthy grains will have to increase. The proper feeding and treatment of animals will draw attention both from groups wishing to make it their cause, and from foodies wanting more flavorful meals. Chefs will be expected to take the lead on more visible social issues such as smaller portion size (to counter obesity) and sustainable organic food (to provide healthy diet choices and reduce the need for harmful fertilizers). Educated parents will feel a responsibility to expose their children to the tastes and benefits of fresh, real foods at an early age, rather than feeding them primarily processed foods or the "treats" available at fast-food restaurants. For those nuclear families who continue to plan less time for regular family dinners, opportunities to practice, explain, and reinforce the benefits of healthier food may be limited.

Getting good value for one's money will remain an important priority for diners, balanced by paying some premium for healthier foods as awareness grows about the long-term impact of food on health. Food critics can play an important role in reinforcing the efforts of enlightened chefs and by praising those who are supporting holistic eating practices. National James Beard awards, the Michelin Guides, and Zagat surveys (all of which currently attract attention from serious foodies) can reinforce this trend through proper recognition of those chefs who embrace the food quality and sustainability practices which hopefully will be demanded in the decades ahead.

Word-of-mouth recommendations will continue to be an ongoing influence on restaurant success. People in the most dedicated "foodie cities" in the United States (such as New York, Chicago, and San Francisco) will continue to eat out often and will be more supportive (and demanding) of their high-end restaurants than diners in other cities. Discerning eaters are more likely to travel greater distances within these cities for a meal they expect will be memorable and unique. This means seeking out not only great gourmet food, but also the more interesting rustic comfort foods cooked by talented chefs. Diners in other cities may continue to view fine dining as primarily for special occasions such as anniversaries and birthdays, which will make it more challenging than ever for high-end gourmet restaurants to survive—let alone thrive—in more sobering recessionary times. Dining is such a subjective experience that a bad meal can dampen any willingness to ever return again to a restaurant. And if the chef is not in the kitchen on a given night, it can sometimes have a negative effect on the quality of the cooking, even if he or she has a well-trained staff.

Who would have thought in 1990 that food would become the primary entertainment for so many people and that chefs would become celebrities as well-known as movie stars? Or that deconstructing traditional recipes and using different temperatures and textures could create so many exciting new flavors and dishes and make gastronomy so intellectually stimulating. The result has been to propel the desire for ongoing, unique dining experiences among so many people. As chefs' spheres of influence expand, people think nothing of traveling to destination restaurants around the world.

The meteoric rise of the new Nordic cooking has primarily been driven by the efforts of Chef Rene Redzepi of Noma in Copenhagen, who has garnered recognition as the number one restaurant in the world in the S.Pellegrino World's 50 Best Restaurants for two years in a row. What is being called "authentic cuisine" utilizes old-fashioned smoking, curing, drying of fresh and cellared vegetables, unripe fruit, and even whey and buttermilk in the cooking. The "Cook it Raw" movement is serious cuisine that disdains recent techniques such as sous vide or deconstructing ingredients as it moves back in time to embrace the natural world of garden scraps (turnip tails, radish leaves, and nasturtium pods) to launch a new era of home-style cooking. It is a huge challenge to make these rustic tastes appealing against the constant onslaught of fast-food choices. It involves finding ways to make age-old basic food relevant again.

In conclusion, several trends appear to be clearly on the cutting edge:

- The desire for healthier food will result in fruits and vegetables being grown and prepared in more interesting ways. Alain Passard at L'Arpege certainly deserves high praise for a successful effort to feature vegetables as the heart of a meal.
- Breakfast will increasingly be regarded as a gourmet meal for some. A trip to Marc Veyrat on Lake Annecy in his prime is only one example of how a great gourmet chef can assem-

ble a selection of incredible choices to satisfy every expectation.

- Ingredients will increasingly be sourced fresh daily from all over the world. In New York, Masa takes this seriously by offering fish and shellfish from more than twenty different locations in his thirty-plus course selection.

- Since people want to experience many different tastes in a meal, small plates will continue to become increasingly popular. Plus, eating smaller portions can have definite health benefits for weight-conscious diners. Some diners have always made appetizers their primary focus, and this now appears to be a full-fledged trend.

- As we become less formal in our dress and manners, a similar trend will emerge in dining. While diners will increasingly resist overly formal venues, they will not accept service that is less rigorous and attentive. Such trends may be disappointing to purists who believe great gourmet dining is one of the highest forms of artistic expression, and for them any compromise in the level of food service or ambiance may not be easily accepted.

Looking back on the last two decades, dining has achieved a level of variety and sophistication no one could have imagined. Why did it happen? Certainly people having more leisure time and discretionary income has encouraged the presentation and consumption of exciting food choices.

For many dedicated eaters, the future of fine dining may be in eating healthier choices at comfortable neighborhood restaurants with informal atmospheres. Those spending more on great food and wine may still have the greatest influence on the ongoing dining revolution by the restaurant choices they make. And finally, with both the commitment and knowledge contributed by increasingly sophisticated chefs and their purveyors, their restaurants will be recognized as the forums for creative expression of their art.

About the Author

BOB MACDONALD has been a serious foodie and wine collector for over forty years. He has eaten at most of the great restaurants in Europe and the United States, and at all twenty-five current Michelin three-star restaurants. Bob completed his undergraduate degree at Kenyon College, earned a law degree at the University of Illinois, and a master's in business administration from the University of Chicago. His early business career included financial positions with Exxon Corporation in New York City, Singapore, and Seattle before moving to the Twin Cities in Minnesota. In 1987, he co-founded the Twin Cities office of the international executive recruiting firm of Russell Reynolds Associates.

Bob is active in the James Beard Foundation, an Officier Commandeur in the Confrerie des Chevaliers du Tastevin and a member of the Commanderie de Bordeaux. He lives in Minneapolis and travels often with his wife Sue, who co-writes the "Bob and Sue's Culinary Adventures" feature on www.andrewzimmern.com.